Reactions to the Third Reich

Then and Now

Harry H. Kahn Memorial Lectures

(2005-2009)

Edited by

Wolfgang Mieder
and
David Scrase

The Center for Holocaust Studies
at the University of Vermont

Burlington, Vermont
2009

ISBN 978-0-9817122-3-9

Manufactured in the United States of America
by Queen City Printers Inc.
Burlington, Vermont

Harry H. Kahn
(1912-1987)

Dedicated to

Prof. David Scrase

founding director of the
Center for Holocaust Studies

and

Professor of German
for almost four decades

at the
University of Vermont

Contents

Preface

Twenty years have passed by since the inaugural Harry H. Kahn Memorial Lecture in 1990. After the fifth annual Kahn Lecture, Prof. Kahn's daughter Hazel Kahn Keimowitz and Wolfgang Mieder edited the book *The Jewish Experience of European Anti-Semitism: Harry H. Kahn Memorial Lectures (1990-1994)* in 1995 with the help of the Department of German and Russian and the Center for Holocaust Studies at the University of Vermont. At that time we decided that we would continue to publish similar books every five years. In 1999 we presented the second volume entitled *Shifting Paradigms in German-Jewish Relations (1750-2000): Harry H. Kahn Memorial Lectures (1995-1999)*, and five years later followed the third volume edited by David Scrase and Wolfgang Mieder with the title *Language, Poetry, and Memory: Reflections on National Socialism: Harry H. Kahn Memorial Lectures (2000-2004)*. And now, yet another five years later, Wolfgang Mieder and David Scrase are in the fortunate position to present the fourth volume with five lectures entitled *Reactions to the Third Reich: Then and Now: Harry H. Kahn Memorial Lectures (2005-2009)*. The five-year cycle of published Kahn essays is solidly established by now, and it is our sincere hope that this will continue to be the case after our retirement from the University of Vermont.

Many students, faculty, staff, and greater Burlington community members have attended these annual lectures by distinguished speakers, and there are some individuals who have been present at all twenty events. But a lecture is not a permanent record, and we are thankful that the fourth group of five lecturers has given us the permission to publish their important papers in yet another volume. The present book is of special significance to us since we invited colleagues and friends from Vermont to share their scholarship with us, namely Professors Frank Nicosia, Mark Stoler, David Scrase, and Helga Schreckenberger as well as Robert Rachlin, a Burlington lawyer and chairperson of the board of the Center for Holocaust Studies at the University of Vermont.

The first five lectures, included in the book mentioned above, were presented by Professors Harry Zohn, Guy Stern, Sander L.

Gilman, Ruth Klüger, and Henri Paucker. The second volume contains the lectures by Professors Egon Schwarz, Karl S. Guthke, Hans Rudolf Vaget, and Doris L. Bergen as well as the address by Madeleine May Kunin, former Governor of Vermont and U.S. Ambassador to Switzerland. The third set of five Kahn lectures were presented by Professors Wolfgang Mieder, Dagmar C.G. Lorenz, Lisa Kahn, Karin Doerr, and Jack Zipes. To this august list of scholars we can now add another group of five experts in German-Jewish cultural, historical, and literary relations, with a special interest in the study and teaching of the Holocaust. The four volumes with their twenty Harry H. Kahn Memorial Lectures contain an intriguing array of studies by major scholars from Canada, Europe, and the United States.

As was the case with the previous three essay volumes, we are once again including the remarks concerning the life and accomplishments of Prof. Harry H. Kahn made by Prof. Wolfgang Mieder as the chairperson of the Department of German and Russian at the inaugural lecture on April 30, 1990. This biographical sketch of the person being honored and remembered with these lectures forms the backdrop to these special annual events on the campus of the University of Vermont. The printed lectures are, as has always been the case, preceded by Prof. Mieder's introductory remarks providing short biographical notes with comments regarding the scholarly accomplishments of the individual speakers.

We would like to thank members of the Kahn family, the Department of German and Russian, and the Center for Holocaust Studies for making the publication of this fourth volume of lectures possible. We hope that this fourth and final volume under our editorship on *Reactions to the Third Reich: Then and Now* will be received with the same positive reaction as was the case with the three earlier books of Harry H. Kahn Memorial Lectures presented at the University of Vermont.

Spring 2009   Wolfgang Mieder
                                              David Scrase

Introduction

At the time of the inauguration of the Harry H. Kahn Memorial Lecture Series on April 30, 1990, at the University of Vermont, members of the Kahn family, friends, students, colleagues, and members of the Burlington community came to pay tribute to the memory of Prof. Harry H. Kahn. The Kahn Lecture is now a treasured annual event. It is especially graitifying that Prof. Kahn's widow Mrs. Irene Kahn, his children and grandchildren as well as other members of the extended Kahn family have made yearly pilgrimages to Vermont to be present at these lectures. In his introductory remarks to each lecture, Prof. Wolfgang Mieder includes a concise biographical sketch of the life and accomplishments of Prof. Harry H. Kahn. The longer version of these laudatory remarks was presented at the inaugural lecture in 1990. They introduced the first essay volume of "Kahn Lectures" in 1995, they were reprinted in the second and third volumes of Kahn Lectures in 1999 and 2004 respectively, and they are included once again in full to keep the memory of our colleague and friend Prof. Harry H. Kahn alive.

When Professor Harry Helmuth Kahn arrived in the United States in 1940 from his native Germany, he had left behind a political regime of intolerance and horror. Under the inhuman policies of the Nazis a dignified existence in the small village of Baisingen in the Black Forest where Harry Kahn was born into a devout Jewish family on June 20, 1912, was no longer possible. In 1936 Harry obtained a master's degree in Education at the University of Würzburg and then taught in the public school system. He also served as the District Supervisor of Jewish schools in Northern Württemberg from 1935 until his forced departure from Germany in 1939. He had escaped the concentration camp and certain death literally at the last moment. His emigration odyssey led him first to England, then a year later to New York, where he married Irene Levi, who also had barely escaped Nazi Germany from the small town of Rexingen only a few miles from Baisingen. The Kahns arrived in Burlington, Vermont, in 1944 and began a new life there for themselves and their daughter Hazel. Max was born a few years later in Burlington. The horrors of the evil Third Reich lay behind them, but Vermont and its landscape were reminiscent of the Black Forest mountains and became a beloved new home for Harry until his death on November 29, 1987.

Upon his arrival in Burlington, Harry became the principal of the Ohavi Zedek Synagogue Hebrew School, and in 1948 he started his employment as an instructor of German at the University of Vermont. In 1951 he earned a second master's degree, in German, from Middlebury College. He became assistant professor at the University of Vermont in 1952, received tenure in 1958, advanced to associate professor in 1969, and became full professor of German in 1974. When Harry Kahn retired in June of 1977, he did so as a highly respected, trusted, and admired chairperson of the Department of German and Russian (spring 1973 and 1975-1976). Realizing what suffering had been brought to his family and friends by the Nazi murderers, one cannot help but admire Harry Kahn's commitment to teaching German language and culture to American students for thirty years. This work must have caused him pain and grief, particularly during the first years of his employment at the University of Vermont. Harry's influence on many students toward a better understanding of this incomprehensible period of tyranny, horror, and death is one of the invaluable contributions he made during his long tenure at this university.

Harry Kahn's commitment to excellence in teaching is legendary. He also gave much time to his Jewish students as the director of Hillel beginning in 1948. In 1952 he succeeded in starting an elementary and intermediate Hebrew program and taught these courses almost until his retirement. The commitment to Harry's Hebrew courses, as they became known, remains very strong, and it is indeed comforting to know that Hebrew, and now also sometimes Yiddish, are being taught in a Department of German and Russian. It is one of Harry's legacies to have made this seemingly absurd combination of languages and cultures possible. It is, of course, also a clear indication that Harry Kahn had a vision throughout his life that perhaps an improved humanity is teachable and attainable.

His vast knowledge of Biblical and modern Hebrew, religion, the history of Judaism, the Old Testament, and philosophy led him to teach courses in the Departments of Religion, Philosophy, and History in addition to his Hebrew and German courses. Who today would, in this age of overspecialization, be able to teach courses at the university level in five disciplines? Harry's drive to gain ever more knowledge in this broad array of fields is well documented by the intellectual rigor of his last sabbatical in the spring of 1974. At the age of sixty-two he enrolled at the Hebrew University of Jerusalem and took courses in Modern Hebrew, Old Testament, the History of Jews in Moslem Countries, and the History of Anti-Semitism.

Upon his retirement, Harry Kahn began to distribute his beloved and huge personal library to his many friends. Many of us have on our shelves books that contain an "ex libris" card inscribed with "Harry and Irene Kahn." Among my treasures are Harry's four volumes of Thomas Mann's *Joseph Stories*, in which literally every page is covered with Harry's detailed notes, comments, and reflections. It is well known that Thomas Mann employed the technique of "leitmotifs" in his novels, and Harry Kahn's marginal comments give us a good idea of what his own guiding "leitmotifs" were.

Those "leitmotifs," which Harry repeatedly noted, include such concepts as "education," "knowledge," "reason," "rationality," "intellect," and "wisdom." While these reflect Harry's sincere commitment to teaching and learning, he also noted again and again that out of this must grow a "consciousness" of "sin" and "guilt," which in turn should lead to an increased "maturity," "responsibility," "justice," and "truth." Harry also often underlined the word "dream" in these novels, and by quoting just a few additional nouns that he or Thomas Mann used on these pages, we sense what this dream was: a "life" full of "tradition," "dignity," "compassion," "beauty," and "love." The Biblical maxim of "faith, hope, (and) love" is a fitting epitaph for this great teacher and scholar. It is his exemplary service to the University of Vermont and the Burlington community as well as his insistence on finding "humanity" even in the gravest and darkest times that are the legacy of our former colleague and friend Professor Harry Helmuth Kahn.

German Zionism and Hitler's Assumption of Power: Between Illusion and Reality

Frank Nicosia

Introduction

The sixteenth annual Harry H. Kahn Memorial Lecture was presented on April 11, 2005, and we were honored to welcome Prof. Frank Nicosia from St. Michael's College at Colchester, Vermont, to the University of Vermont. He is a frequent guest on our campus, and we appreciate his interest in our German and Holocaust programs.

It is a special delight to welcome our distinguished colleague and good friend Prof. Frank Nicosia from St. Michael's College to the campus of the University of Vermont. As an historian, he received his B.A. degree from Pennsylvania State University in 1967, and after spending a year in the Peace Corps in Libya, he earned his M.A. degree from Georgetown University of 1969. From 1971 to 1973 he taught at the Peter Dörfler Gymnasium at Marktoberdorf/Allgäu, Germany, and then settled in Montreal where he finished his Ph.D. degree in 1978 at McGill University. He did some teaching at Concordia University in Montreal and Dalhousie University in Halifax during this time, but in 1979 St. Michael's College was fortunate to attract Prof. Frank Nicosia as an historian to its campus.

While Prof. Nicosia is a renowned faculty member at St. Michael's College, he also has a considerable presence at the University of Vermont. Since the founding of our Center for Holocaust Studies, he has been an influential member of its advisory board, he has taught in our summer course on the Holocaust, and he has contributed chapters on "The Emergence of Modern Anti-semitism in Germany and Europe" (1996), "Zionism, Anti-semitism, and the Coming of the Final Solution" (2001), and "A German Diplomat and the Fate of the German Jews: The case of

Heinrich Wolff" (2004) to three essay volumes published by the
UVM Center for Holocaust Studies. In addition, he attends numerous Holocaust related events on this campus, just as we par-
ticipate in the numerous programs sponsored by St. Michael's
College. Prof. Nicosia is thus an invaluable ambassador between
our two schools, and I am certain that my colleagues and our students would agree with me that his commitment to Holocaust
scholarship and education has earned him the distinction to be an
honorary member of the UVM community.

It is not possible to enumerate all of his publications, but let
me mention his two significant books on *The Third Reich and the
Palestine Question* (1985) and *The Columbia Guide to the Holocaust* (2000), co-authored with Donald Niewyk. He is also the editor of two volumes on *The Central Zionist Archives Jerusalem,
1933-1938 / 1939-1945* (1990), and the co-editor with *Lawrence
Stokes of Germans Against Nazism: Nonconformity, Opposition
and Resistance in the Third Reich* (1990). But there are also three
very important books of the proceedings of the Miller symposia
sponsored by the UVM Center for Holocaust Studies every two
years. Together with our colleague Prof. Jonathan Huener from
the Department of History, Prof. Nicosia has edited the three volumes on *Medicine and Medical Ethics in Nazi Germany: Origins,
Practices, Legacies* (2002), *Business and Industry in Nazi Germany* (2004), and *The Arts in Nazi Germany* (2006). These essay
volumes contain publications by major international Holocaust
scholars, and their insights have reached many libraries and above
all students because of the relatively low purchasing price of the
paperback editions. In addition, the collaborative editorial work
by professors Nicosia and Huener serves, of course, as yet another sign of the cooperative work between St. Michael's College
and the University of Vermont.

As expected, Prof. Nicosia's *curriculum vitae* also lists nu-
merous articles that have appeared in such prestigious journals as
*Canadian Journal of History, Journal of Modern History, Leo
Baeck Institute Yearbook, International Journal of Middle East
Studies, History of European Ideas, Journal of Contemporary
History, Holocaust and Genocide Studies*, and *Vierteljahrshefte
für Zeitgeschichte*. In fact, due to his superb knowledge of the
German language, Prof. Nicosia published his article in the last

journal mentioned in German with the title of "Ein nützlicher Feind: Zionismus im nationalsozialistischen Deutschland, 1933-1939." This particular article shows, of course, the importance of foreign languages in the serious study of the Holocaust.

Having gained an international reputation through his informed and insightful scholarship, Prof. Nicosia has frequently been called upon to submit entries to the *Encyclopedia of the Holocaust*, the *Encyclopedia of the Modern Middle East*, the *Encyclopedia of Science, Technology, and Ethics*, and the *Encyclopedia of Genocide and Crimes Against Humanity*. Obviously Prof. Nicosia has also presented numerous lectures at national and international conferences, and his meticulous research has been supported by major grants from the U.S. Holocaust Memorial Museum, the Fulbright Commission, the American Philosophical Society, the Deutscher Akademischer Austauschdienst, the American Council of Learned Societies, and the National Endowment of the Humanities. Finally, I would also like to mention Prof. Nicosia's dedicated service to the German Studies Association that serves as an umbrella organization for the study of German culture, history, language, literature, and politics.

We have every reason to feel fortunate to have such a recognized educator and scholar in the greater Burlington area. He has dedicated his scholarly life to the teaching and study of the Holocaust, and he has touched students on both our campuses. For all of his diligent and dedicated work we owe him much thanks and appreciation.

Lecture

Introduction

First, allow me to thank the Department of German and Russian and the Center for Holocaust Studies for the honor of giving this year's sixteenth annual Harry Kahn lecture. And thanks to UVM for the opportunity over the past twelve years to work with wonderful colleagues at the Center for Holocaust Studies, including David Scrase, Jonathan Huener, Wolfgang Mieder, and Kathy Johnson, and with the entire Advisory Board. It has been an honor and opportunity for me, and an awful lot of fun as well.

I never knew Harry Kahn, but I wish I had. Wolfgang wrote in the Introduction to the first volume of Kahn lectures that Harry Kahn insisted "on finding humanity even in the gravest and darkest times."[1] Professor Kahn was right to do so, of course, although as a historian of this period, I have never found that to be an easy task. But I will attempt to do that in my talk today.

The substance of my lecture is taken from the first two chapters of the book manuscript I hope to complete this summer on the relationship between Zionism and anti-Semitism in the Third Reich. Much of it is from the first chapter that considers the ideological relationship between German anti-Semitism and German Zionism during the age of Jewish emancipation in Germany, i.e. before 1933. Part of it is from the second chapter that deals with the first year of Nazi rule, 1933, a year in which both the Nazis and the Zionists seemed to entertain illusions about each other. My focus today is on the Zionist side of that relationship. I have been intrigued by the almost prophetic nature of the Zionist argument within the Jewish community in Germany before 1933 about the futility of Jewish assimilation in Germany, and the inevitable triumph of anti-Semitism. And there was some of the "we told you so" attitude in the Zionist position during the years immediately after 1945 as Jews and non-Jews tried to comprehend the destruction of two-thirds of Europe's Jews during the Second World War.

But the thrust of this particular aspect of my project, and of my talk today, is the premise that Zionists in Germany, in spite of the logic of their arguments about the nature of modern anti-Semitism, in the end had no better grasp of the nature of National Socialism and its anti-Semitism than anyone else, Jews non-Jews. I do not intend this as criticism or an accusation; it is merely a sad reality

In the turbulent months preceding Hitler's appointment as German chancellor, Zionists, as all Jews in Germany, struggled to determine the nature of the crisis they might face. Their assessments of the possibility of a National Socialist assumption of power ranged mostly from the conviction that Hitler would never make it into the government, to assertions that even if he did, it would not necessarily spell disaster for Germany's Jews, certainly not if a Zionist solution to the Jewish question in Germany were possible. There were few doomsday predictions. These fluctuations reflected the wishful thinking that prevailed in the larger constellation of anti-Nazi forces in the early 1930s. Again, I don't intend this as criticism of those Jews and non-Jews in Germany who failed to foresee the disaster that was coming, for they obviously did not have the hindsight that we possess today.

What today appears as an illusory view of the future, one that seemed to characterize German Zionists before the Nazi assumption of power, was conditioned by two factors: an ideologically interdependent relationship between Zionism and anti-Semitism before 1933; and ambivalence in Zionist policies and politics during the Weimar years, both within and beyond the German-Jewish community, with regard to National Socialism.

Before the establishment of the state of Israel in 1948, overt, active anti-Zionism, which many today condemn as a manifestation of anti-Semitism, was essentially a Jewish phenomenon, a struggle that was largely confined to Jewish communities in the Diaspora. There was relatively little opposition to Zionism among non-Jews. In fact, most non-Jewish assessments of Zionism, particularly before 1914, tended to be favorable. It was motivated by a variety of factors, including the anti-Semitism of nationalist and racist ideologues and politicians who recognized their common acceptance of the national distinctiveness of the Jews and the desirability of separating Jews from non-Jews. In Germany, there was a convergence of interests between Zionists and anti-Semites in reversing Jewish assimilation and promoting Jewish emigration. The Zionist concept of the Jews as a distinct *Volk*, properly belonging in its own homeland in Palestine, appealed to anti-Semites who shared with the Zionists the conviction that Jews were Jewish by nationality, that they were not German, and that they should leave Germany.

On the other hand, in Germany and elsewhere one found the most vehement and virulent opposition to the Zionist idea among Jews. Countless examples exist, ranging from the Munich Jewish community's refusal to permit the first international Zionist congress to meet in that city in 1897 (it had to move to Basel) to the many virulently anti-Zionist comments that Victor Klemperer makes in his wartime diaries. One example is his entry of 22 April 1935 in which, after meeting with Kurt Blumenfeld, the German

Zionist leader from 1924 to 1933, Klemperer observes: "The Blu-
menfelds were here on Friday; I disagree violently with him about
Zionism, which he defends and praises, which I call betrayal and
Hitlerism."[2]

The rise of modern Zionism in Europe in the late nineteenth
century occurred primarily on two parallel tracks. On the one
hand, there were the dominant, secular political Zionists such as
Moses Hess, Leon Pinsker, Theodor Herzl, and others who responded to the immediacy of modern anti-Semitism. In his speech
to the First International Zionist Congress in Basel in 1897, Herzl
stated: "Only the hatred has made us foreigners again in our own
lands, and only that hatred will make us a nation again."[3] The cultural Zionists, on the other hand, represented by the likes of Asher
Ginsburg (Achad-Ha'am), Martin Buber, and others, believed that
the disintegration of Jewish cultural distinctiveness under the
combined impact of civic emancipation and secular enlightenment was the primary cause of the so-called "Jewish problem."
Achad-Ha'am noted: "The Jews cannot survive...now that our
spiritual isolation is ended because we no longer have any defense
against the ocean of foreign culture that threatens to obliterate our
national characteristics and traditions."[4] For the political Zionists,
the problem was primarily rejection in the form of hatred and persecution; for the cultural Zionists it was mainly acceptance, in the
form of Jewish assimilation. Of course, for all of them, in the end,
it was both. In his speech to the first international Zionist congress
in Basel in 1897, Max Nordau argued that in aspiring to acceptance and assimilation, the Jews alienated themselves from their
own roots and natural community, only to be callously rejected by
gentile society.[5] In both cases, early Zionists articulated a fundamental premise of both political and cultural Zionism that National Socialism ultimately would not dispute, namely that Jewish
emancipation and assimilation were causes of — rather than solutions to — the so-called Jewish problem.[6]

The second explanation for Zionist illusions on the eve of the
Nazi Machtübernahme is the ambivalence of Zionist politics with
regard to the intensification of anti-Semitism and the developing
Nazi threat during the Weimar years, an ambivalence that arises
out of its ideological interdependence with anti-Semitism. In the
era after World War I, with the Palestine Mandate and the Jewish

National Home in place, the German Zionist federation was inclined to refrain from Jewish self-defense (*jüdische Abwehr*) against anti-Semitism, something that the larger non-Zionist Jewish organizations in Germany, particularly the Central Association of German Citizens of the Jewish Faith (Centralverein deutscher Staatsbürger jüdischen Glaubens, or CV) pursued with vigor. The Zionists preferred to concentrate their energies and resources on preparing Jews for emigration to and settlement in Palestine. Kurt Blumenfeld, the long-time president of the German Zionist federation, would later write of that early strategy: "We expected nothing from the formal civic equality of the Jews in Germany."[7] Besides their focus on Palestine, German Zionists concentrated their efforts on winning over German Jews for the Zionist idea. Their struggle was within the Jewish community; they considered the struggle against anti-Semitism as the natural, albeit futile, work of the larger non-Zionist German Jewish organizations.

A year before Hitler's appointment as chancellor, and some seven months before the Nazi electoral success of July 1932, Kurt Blumenfeld wrote to Chaim Weizmann, president of the World Zionist Organization in London, insisting that it was unlikely that Hitler would ever come to power.[8] Although he admitted that a Nazi coup was conceivable, he expressed confidence that president von Hindenburg would never appoint Hitler as chancellor. He noted that the Zionist movement was making progress in Germany in the face of continued opposition from the larger non-Zionist and anti-Zionist Jewish organizations. In August 1932, at perhaps the lowest ebb of Germany's economic and political crisis, the Zionist newspaper *Jüdische Rundschau* published an editorial entitled *Hitler Reichskanzler?* (Hitler Reich Chancellor?)[9] A curious mix of illusion and reality, it reassured its readers that a Hitler government would not necessarily mean that Nazi racial tenets would become law in Germany. While it did warn that German Jewry was possibly entering a new and difficult era, the editorial tried to reassure its readers that Hitler's appointment as chancellor would mean the complete collapse of the "assimilationist mentality of German Jews." Earlier that summer, Blumenfeld had written to Weizmann that the deepening crisis could motivate many more Jews to embrace Zionism.[10]

In 1932, therefore, German Zionists did not dwell on specific actions a Nazi government might take against the Jews in Germany; nor did they really concern themselves with self-defense activities designed to work against a Nazi political victory.[11] Rather they continued to stress the correctness of the traditional Zionist message, the failure of most German Jews to heed that message in the past, and the singular importance for Jews of Zionism's role in any future upheaval. Again, looking back on those unsettling times, Blumenfeld would later write that the Zionists were the only Jews in Germany who recognized the danger by spiritually and materially preparing for the exodus from Germany, as opposed to fighting the inevitable. He noted: "Deep down I felt from the bottom of my heart that the fundamental lie of Jewish life in Germany had to be eliminated."[12]

On 20 January 1933, just ten days before Hitler's appointment as chancellor, the German Zionist Federation reiterated its approach to the political uncertainties in Germany at the time.[13] Affirming the correctness of the Zionist solution to the Jewish question in Germany, the statement argued that the Jews were not in a position to understand the new realities in German life because they always foolishly expected the solution to the Jewish question to come with their full acceptance into German society. It concluded: "There is nothing left for the Jews but to be Jews, and to distance themselves from the non-Jewish world." This approach was also taken time and again by the *Jüdische Rundschau* in its editorials, especially during the early weeks of the Nazi regime, when it was not at all clear exactly what Hitler's government had in store for the Jewish community.[14] If anything, the uncertainty reinforced traditional Zionist warnings about the futility of assimilation and the durability of anti-Semitism, and that the approaching Nazi reality could create unprecedented opportunity for Zionist success within a Jewish community that had been traditionally hostile to Zionism.

In all of this, German Zionists naturally assumed that the conditions of Jewish life created by Jewish emancipation before 1933 would continue as the essential environment for effective Zionist work for as long as Jews remained in Germany. Although they had rejected emancipation as the realistic solution to the Jewish question, they had always recognized its essential role in the task of preparing Jews for Palestine. Despite their general aversion to self-defense against anti-Semitism before 1933, the *Jüdische Rundschau* had greeted the revolution in Germany back in November 1918 with the words: "Democracy and Justice, under whose sign the German people are entering the new era, are strong and lasting supports for us. We welcome the revolution!"[15] The 15th Congress of the German Zionist organization in December 1918, clearly stressed the twin goals of building up the Jewish National Home in Palestine and the complete equality of Jews in Germany and in other countries.[16] And, in the waning months of the Weimar Republic, German Zionists appreciated even more that emancipation remained an essential means to the fulfillment of Zionist ends.[17] As it contemplated its own critical role in the gathering storm in 1932, the German Zionist Federation was forced to confront the reality that a Nazi government might pursue policies that would undermine an environment of emancipation, the only environment conducive to effective Zionist work in Germany. In apparent contradiction to the policy of non-involvement in self defense against anti-Semitism, the September 1932 resolution of the Frankfurt *Delegiertentag* on the position of Jews in Germany called for a Zionist "...struggle to promote our demands — the guarantee of equality and freedom, and the development of our separate identity — with all our strength."[18]

Attempts at Accommodation

Before January 30th, 1933, German Zionists did not preclude the necessity of discussions with a possible future National Socialist state.[19] Thereafter, they tried to convince Nazi authorities of the need to maintain suitable living conditions for Jews in Germany, including protection of their civil rights and of their economic livelihood, until the process of emigration ran its course. On June 21, 1933, the German Zionist organization addressed a formal declaration to Hitler expressing its desire to work for the resolution of the Jewish question in Germany in a manner that would be in the best interests of both the German and the Jewish peoples. Entitled "Statement of the Zionist Federation for Germany on the Position of the Jews in the New German State," it rejected emancipation and assimilation as solutions to the Jewish question. It formally endorsed Germany's national rebirth under National Socialism and the principles on which it was based: ethnic or racial descent (*volkische Abstammung*), religion, the common destiny of the German people (*Schicksalsgemeinschaft*), and the German consciousness of national uniqueness (*Artbewusstsein*) that were its foundations and that were, as the statement reiterated, the foundations of Zionism as the expression of the national rebirth of the Jewish people.[20] The statement concluded by proposing a protected minority status for the Jewish community while the process of emigration was under way.

If this statement was rather vague about the specific conditions under which German Jews might live in the new Germany, an internal German Zionist Federation memorandum of 13 September, 1933 addressed that question with considerable clarity and detail.[21] Its author, Martin Rosenblüth, reasoned that German Zionism had little choice but to seek conditions that would ensure an orderly Jewish emigration, and that those conditions, especially the matter of the assets of the emigrants, were possible only with the cooperation and support of Nazi authorities. This kind of pragmatism is obviously part of the reason for the 21 June endorsement of Nazi efforts to build a racial state. Rosenblüth defined a specific status for Jews in the new Germany that should prevail during an orderly emigration process, and called for the civil and legal equality of Jews and the avoidance of any restrictions on their economic livelihood. While his appeal for support from the state for the occupational training of young Jews to prepare them for a new life in Palestine, and for protection of autonomous Jewish religious institutions, schools, sports organizations, welfare agencies and emigration offices would in fact be realized, his plea for the emigration of German Jews with their assets was unacceptable to the Nazis. In short, Rosenblüth hoped that the means to the common end of Jewish emigration would be characterized by conditions of Jewish life in Germany not unlike those that prevailed before 1933, with the understanding that they would be temporary rather than permanent.

The small, rightist Revisionist State Zionist Organization (*Staatszionistische Organisation*) entertained similar illusions about a meeting of the minds with Hitler's government regarding Jewish policy. A 1935 position paper made a similar argument about the convergence of interests between the Nazi state, the German people, and Zionism.[22] In an argument similar to the June

21 statement of the German Zionist Federation, the position paper endorsed Nazi aims to build a new Germany in which its *völkisch* principles excluded the Jews from participation: "The Jews living in Germany recognize the right of the German people to form its own national life that will exclude all undesirable mixing of peoples...they reject any propaganda and resistance against the measures undertaken by the German government...for the solution of the Jewish question."

The Zionists also moved to take over the leadership of German Jewry. On April 20, 1933, Blumenfeld urged the members of the German Zionist Federation to seize the initiative and win over Germany's Jews to Zionism with the words: "Nevertheless there exists today a very real opportunity to win over German Jewry to the Zionist idea."[23] By the end of October, the German Zionist Federation announced: "We rightfully claim for the Zionist movement the leadership of internal Jewish life. A pre-condition for this is for our movement to spread throughout a German Jewry that is ripe for Zionism, and which can be won through the systematic application of our energies."[24]

But the anti-Semitism of the regime, something Zionists traditionally believed they understood, would preclude most of Rosenblüth's program, and impose extraordinarily difficult conditions that would impede Zionist efforts to secure an orderly and economically viable Jewish emigration. About the only positive result of these developments was a growing interest in Zionism among German Jews, as the regime vigorously banned statements, activities, policies, etc. that counseled Jews to remain in Germany. The work of the three major non-Zionist Jewish organizations was dramatically curtailed, and they receded into political oblivion.

The end of 1933 brought with it the realization that Hitler was not simply a passing phenomenon, and that the conditions of emancipation under which Zionists had been able to work in the past were ending. There would continue to be periodic but futile attempts by Zionist and non-Zionist organizations inside and outside of Germany to convince Nazi authorities that the best way to facilitate Jewish emigration was to allow the Jews some degree of economic freedom and subsistence until they were able to emigrate.

Reality: The End of Emancipation

Let me now turn to the reality that set in for German Zionists by the end of 1933. Zionist hopes that the regime might afford German Jews some protection until an orderly Jewish emigration could be completed were never realized. Beyond the opportunity to take a small portion of their assets with them if they emigrated to Palestine, and support for Zionist occupational retraining programs in Germany for young Jews going to Palestine, Zionists were not spared the arbitrary treatment and brutality meted out to all Jews in Germany during the 1930s.[25] Reports from Berlin by German Zionists told of raids by storm troopers on Zionist headquarters in which telephone wires were cut, cupboards forced open, petty cash and postage stamps stolen, and documents taken away. There were even harshly anti-Zionist articles in the *Völkischer Beobachter* and other Nazi publications.[26] The World Zionist Organization in London chronicled arrests, beatings, abductions, and even a few murders.[27] Zionists were not spared the arbitrary treatment meted out to the so-called "assimilationist" Jewish organizations, and they joined non-Zionists is asking Jewish leaders abroad to moderate or even cancel the anti-German rallies and economic boycotts that they believed were contributing to anti-Jewish persecution in Germany.[28]

The end of Jewish emancipation, therefore, had devastating consequences for Zionist work in Germany after 1933. The inevitable realities of Nazi anti-Jewish policies, especially the impoverishment of the entire Jewish community, the breakdown of communal relations within the Jewish community, the disintegration of cohesion and authority within the German Zionist leadership, and the isolation of the German Zionist movement from the larger international Zionist movement, precluded the kind of reeducation and emigration process that the Zionists had always desired.

1. Economic Deprivation

By the end of 1935, more than a quarter of the Jews in Germany were destitute. Even before legislation in 1938 that would complete the process of removing the Jews from the German economy, the Jewish community had been crushed economically.[29] The steady erosion of the economic position of Jews was in many ways the most difficult burden with which the German Zionist organization and other Jewish organizations had to deal, even with the extraordinary self-help efforts of the entire Jewish community.[30] Michael Traub, the Director of the Palestine Foundation Fund (Keren Hajessod) in Germany, observed in October, 1933,: "Regarding the situation in Germany, it can only be said in a letter that the process of economic deprivation which is inexorably and systematically being pursued is worse than all acts of violence."[31] Zionist educational and occupational retraining programs were increasingly difficult to organize and fund, immigration certificates for Palestine not always easy to obtain, and the anticipated orderly transfer of Jews and their assets to Palestine was, in relative terms, minimal, and by no means orderly or complete.

2. Communal Relations

Nazi policies tended to exacerbate rather than neutralize the long-standing conflicts between the Zionists and other Jewish organizations in Germany. Traditional differences and rivalries were placed in a different and more dangerous context as the state declared all Jews to be the enemy, and indirectly forced the various Jewish organizations to attempt to create a single Jewish response. The formation in September 1933 of the Reich Representation of German Jews (Reichsvertretung der deutschen Juden), an umbrella organization through which major Jewish organizations would attempt to speak with one voice, ultimately was not successful in ameliorating traditional conflicts. This closer proximity of Jewish organizations in the face of common adversity did not in the end resolve old conflicts.[32] The difficult relationship between the German Zionist Federation and the once dominant, non-Zionist Central Association of German Citizens of the Jewish Faith (CV) that existed before 1933 continued more or less unchanged thereafter.[33] Even after its grudging realization by the end of 1935, with the promulgation of the Nuremberg Racial Laws, that Jewish life in Germany was ending and Jewish emigration was the only option for German Jews, the CV criticized what it believed to be Zionist efforts to direct Jewish emigration exclusively to Palestine at the expense of other suitable destinations.[34] The CV also resented Zionist claims to leadership over the German Jewish community, and refused to cede to the Zionist Federation any sort of leadership role.[35] The new realities in Jewish life in Germany after 1933 also threw the Zionists and the Reich Association of Jewish War Veterans (Reichsbund jüdischer Frontsoldaten) into a conflict that reflected all of the bitterness of the traditional Zionist-non-Zionist struggle among Jews in Germany since the late nineteenth century.[36] The fiercely anti-Zionist, *deutschnationale*, League of National German Jews (Verband nationaldeutscher Juden) would have nothing to do with the Zionists before it was dissolved by the authorities in 1935. But without question the Zionist Federation's most bitterly contentious relationship after 1933 was with the revisionist Zionist movement in Germany where the new realities greatly increased the stakes in an already acrimonious competition for the allegiance of all Jews, particularly the Zionists. This even resulted in legal proceedings in Palestine in 1937 against the leadership of the Revisionist movement in Germany, which stood accused of conspiring to destroy the German Zionist Federation.[37]

3. Internal Dissolution

The combination of rapid growth, the harsh anti-Jewish measures of the regime, and the inability of the organization to deal with that combination forced the German Zionist Federation to face insurmountable difficulties.[38] A major problem was the loss of experienced Zionist leaders and activists who emigrated to Palestine in ever greater numbers after 1933, at a time when they were needed in Germany to cope with the sudden growth of the Zionist movement. In 1933 alone, prominent Zionist leaders such as Kurt Blumenfeld and Georg Landauer emigrated to Palestine, and Martin Rosenblüth left for England.[39] In 1935, Robert Weltsch, editor of the *Jüdische Rundschau*, wrote with regret from Berlin to Jerusalem that: "The departure of leading Zionist personalities is having a negative impact."[40] It became a particularly acute problem after the *Kristallnacht* pogrom of November, 1938, as Benno Cohn reported in a letter from Berlin to Jerusalem: "Once again the problem of personnel...is very difficult. At this time, all want to leave and there is hardly anyone to take over."[41] Although the early removal of Jewish teachers from the German school system had created a glut of teachers for private Jewish schools in the early years of the Nazi regime, these schools soon experienced a crippling teacher shortage as more and more Jewish teachers and school administrators emigrated.[42]

4. Isolation

The German Zionist movement became increasingly isolated from the larger world Zionist movement after 1936. Contact between the German Zionist Federation and the Jewish Agency in London and Jerusalem became more infrequent and more difficult to maintain. In October, 1936, the German Zionist Federation complained to the Jewish Agency that German Zionists were virtually cut off from information concerning political activities in Palestine and in the larger Zionist movement world-wide, which impeded the effectiveness of their work in Germany.[43] In 1937, it further complained to the Jewish Agency that most of its publications and correspondence were in now English and Hebrew, and no longer in German, arguing that this was not practical since millions of Jews in central and eastern Europe spoke German but not English or Hebrew.[44] By July, 1938, Franz Meyer of the German Zionist Federation wrote to the Jewish Agency office in London lamenting the fact that the views of German Zionists were not solicited for the Jewish Agency's formal memorandum to the international conference on refugees at Evian in 1938. A few days later, Meyer wrote to London: "I beg you to make every effort in the future, in spite of the existing impediments, not to desist from sending us all necessary materials."[45]

Conclusion:

Impoverishment, communal conflict, internal disintegration, and international isolation: these realities were not conducive to successful Zionist work in Germany after the Nazi assumption of power in 1933. It is true that some 53,000 German Jews (about 10% of all Jews living in Germany in 1933) were able to leave for Palestine between 1933 and 1941. This represents about 53,000 potential victims of the Final Solution who were saved. It is undoubtedly something to celebrate; but it is a far cry from what Zionists anticipated would be the natural result of the encounter between anti-Semitism and Zionism in central Europe. Over time, they believed, Germans and Jews alike would come to accept the logic of Zionism and the mutual benefits of what Herzl called a "modern solution to the Jewish question" in the sub-title of his book, *The Jewish State*. Moreover, all would work in an environment that would permit the peaceful reeducation of German Jews and their orderly departure from Germany with much of their assets.

It would seem, then, that many of the early Zionists did not understand the real nature of modern anti-Semitism; nor were they able to anticipate its application as state policy under National Socialism. They were certainly not alone. But unlike the majority of so-called "assimilationist" Jews in Germany, Zionists in general tended to view the anti-Semitism around them as the normal, inevitable byproduct of Jewish emancipation, as something to be accommodated rather than resisted if it was to be eliminated. Out of this apparent convergence of interests with anti-Semitism, an accommodation was supposed to amount to a mutual — even if not always easy or cordial — effort to end Jewish assimilation and promote Jewish emigration

Before 1933, Zionists claimed that the majority non-Zionist Jews in Germany were living an illusion, namely that Jews could overcome anti-Semitism and be both German and Jewish in Germany. Zionists believed that was impossible, and that they could be Jews only in their own state in Palestine. But if the so-called "assimilationists" were living an illusion, the Zionists were undoubtedly living one of their own. It was the fallacy that since anti-Semitism was understandable, indeed inevitable, as Herzl and others asserted, there was room for some sort of accommodation with Zionism. Herzl wrote in *The Jewish State*: "I believe I understand anti-Semitism. I regard this movement as a Jew, but without hatred and fear."[46] He believed that anti-Semites would accept Zionism, that they would do everything necessary to support it until they reached the common goal of removing Jews from Germany.

What Herzl and other Zionists of his day did not understand, and what post-World War I German Zionists apparently would not understand, was that the appeal of Zionism for most anti-Semites, particularly for the Nazis after World War I, was of a purely practical nature: Zionist willingness to exclude the Jews from the German *Volksgemeinschaft* (racial community), to promote a Jewish national consciousness and, ultimately, emigration from Germany, could be nothing more than a useful instrument to help rid Germany of a "problem;" it could not be indicative of anything positive or redemptive in Jewish life that would benefit the German people. Therefore, it could never be worthy of positive support. Indeed, many considered Zionism to be representative of much of what they considered to be the more dangerous and abhorrent characteristics of the Jews as a people. The Zionist determination to remain Jewish and to promote a Jewish consciousness and identity, while welcomed in the practical sense of reversing Jewish assimilation and encouraging emigration, nevertheless sharpened the focus ideologically on the object of their hatred — the Jews themselves. For instance, anti-Semitic myths of an historical world Jewish conspiracy formed the basis of the fierce condemnation in the Nazi government and press of the Zionist aim to establish an independent Jewish state in Palestine. The simple utility of Zionism in the implementation of policies derived from fundamental anti-Semitic ideology could never be a basis for the kind of reasonable collaboration the Zionists had anticipated. For Zionists were, like the "assimilationists," still Jews; they were therefore inseparable from the object of Nazi hatred and intent.

Georg Landauer, Director in Jerusalem of the Central Bureau for the Settlement of German Jews in Palestine and former General Secretary of the German Zionist Federation before his emigration to Palestine in 1933, returned to Berlin for a brief visit in February 1939. In a long letter to a colleague in Jerusalem, he described the situation for Jews in Germany as grim, and the conditions for Zionist work as virtually impossible.[47] Counting Austria and the Sudetenland, there were still some 400,000 Jews in Greater Germany. Besides the impoverishment of those Jews who remained in Germany, and the consequent problems it created for the emigration process, Landauer focused on the extraordinary difficulties in effectively carrying out Zionist work since 1933, difficulties that had been a consequence of Nazi policy. He saw little hope of completing the task of moving Jews out of Germany to Palestine. In a somber, somewhat prophetic vein, a tacit recognition that previous assumptions had not materialized, Landauer closed with the following words:

Die Stimmung der Juden in Deutschland ist unbeschreiblich
bedrückt. Sie wissen wirklich keinen Ausweg und warten darauf,
was die Regierung mit ihnen anfangen wird. Arbeitslager? Ande-
re Methoden der Liquidierung?

(The mood of the Jews in Germany is one of indescribable de-
jection. They really know of no way out, and they wait to see what
the government will do with them. Work camps? Other methods
of liquidation?)

Notes:
[1] Hazel Kahn Keimowitz and Wolfgang Mieder (eds.), *The
Jewish Experience of Anti-Semitism. Harry H. Kahn Memorial
Lectures 1990-1994* (Burlington: University of Vermont, 1995), x.

[2] Victor Klemperer, *Ich will Zeugnis ablegen bis zum letzten:
Tagebücher 1933-1941* (Berlin Aufbau Verlag, 1995), 193.

[3] Shulamit Volkov, *Jüdisches Leben und Antisemitismus im
19. und 20. Jahrhundert* (Munich: C.H. Beck, 1990), 96.

[4] Gideon Shimoni, *The Zionist Ideology* (Hanover: University Press of New England, 1995),105

[5] Zionistische Aktionskomitee (ed.), *Max Nordau's Zionistische Schriften*, Kongressrede, Basel, 29. August 1897 (Cologne
and Leipzig: Jüdischer Verlag, 1909), 50-51.

[6] See for example Theodor Herzl, *Der Judenstaat. Versuch
einer modernen Lösung der Judenfrage*, in Julius Schoeps
(Hrsg.), *Wenn Ihr Wollt, ist es kein Märchen* (Königstein/Ts:
Jüdischer Verlag bei Athenäum, 1985), 209-211.

[7] Kurt Blumenfeld, *Erlebte Judenfrage: Ein Vierteljahrhun-
dert Deutscher Zionismus* (Stuttgart: Deutsche Verlags-Anstalt,
1962), 189.

[8] Central Zionist Archives, Jerusalem (hereafter CZA):
A222/24, Kurt Blumenfeld, Berlin to Chaim Weizmann, London,
5 January 1932, reprinted in Kurt Blumenfeld, *Im Kampf um den
Zionismus: Briefe aus fünf Jahrzehnten* (Stuttgart: Deutsche Verlags-Anstalt, 1976), 114-118.

[9] *Jüdische Rundschau*, 12. August 1932, reprinted in Jehuda
Reinharz, *Dokumente zur Geschichte des deutschen Zionismus*,
Schriftenreihe wissenschaftlicher Abhandlungen des Leo Baeck

Instituts 37 (Tübingen: Mohr/Siebeck, 1981), Nr. 210, 528-530.

[10] Kurt Blumenfeld, *Im Kampf um den Zionismus: Briefe aus fünf Jahrzeiten* (Stuttgart: Deutsche Verlags-Anstalt, 1976), 122.

[11] For the ambiguous relationship between the ZVfD and the idea of defence against Antisemitism in Weimar Germany, see: Arnold Paucker, *Der jüdische Abwehrkampf gegen Antisemitismus und Nationalsozialismus in den letzten Jahren der Weimarer Republik* (Hamburg: Leibnitz, 1969), 39 ff; Jehuda Reinharz, "The Zionist Response to Antisemitism in Germany", *Leo Baeck Institute Year Book* 30 (1985), 105-140.

[12] Blumenfeld, *Erlebte Judenfrage*, 186.

[13] For the full text of this statement, see Ibid., 203-204.

[14] See for example *Jüdische Rundschau*, 31. Januar 1933; 29. März 1933.

[15] *Jüdische Rundschau*, 15. November 1918, as cited in Werner T. Angress, "Juden im politischen Leben der Revolutionszeit", in Werner E. Mosse (ed.), *Deutsches Judentum in Krieg und Revolution 1916-1923*, Schriftenreihe Wissenschaftlicher Abhandlungen des Leo Baeck Instituts 25 (Tübingen: Mohr/Siebeck, 1971), 146.

[16] 'Protokoll des XV. Delegiertentages der Zionistischen Vereinigung für Deutschland', Berlin, den 25.-27. Dezember 1918, reprinted in Reinharz, *Dokumente*, Nr. 116, 245-254.

[17] This idea is touched upon briefly in Francis R. Nicosia, "Ein nützlicher Feind. Zionismus im nationalsozialistischen Deutschland 1933-1939", *Vierteljahrshefte für Zeitgeschichte* 37 (1989), 367-400. For an excellent account of the larger implications of the end of emancipation for Jews in Germany in the 1930's, see Reinhard Rürup, "Das Ende der Emanzipation: Die antijüdische Politik in Deutschland von der 'Machtergreifung' bis zum Zweiten Weltkrieg", in Arnold Paucker (ed.), *Die Juden im Nationalsozialistischen Deutschland / The Jews in Nazi Germany 1933-1943*, Schriftenreihe wissenschaftlicher Abhandlungen des Leo Baeck Instituts 45 (Tübingen: Mohr/Siebeck, 1986), 97-114.

[18] *Jüdische Rundschau*, 21 Oktober 1932. See also the minutes of the meeting of the Landesvorstand (state board of directors) of the ZVfD in Berlin of January 8, 1933, in Reihharz, *Dokumente*, Nr. 214, 545-552.

[19] Blumenfeld, *Im Kampf*, 122.

[20] Politischcs Archiv des Auswäitigen Amts, Berlin (hereafter PA): Inland II A/B, 83-21, Bd.1, "Äusserung der Zionistischen Vereinigung für Deutschland zur Stellung der Juden im neuen deutschen Staat," Berlin, 21. Juni 1933.

[21] PA: Ref.D., Po5 NE adh 6, Nr. 4, Bd.2, "Zusätzliche Bemerkungen zur deutschen Judenfrage," 13. September 1933 These remarks were the second part of his larger report on the outcome of the Eighteenth Zionist Congress which had just concluded in Prague. It is likely that this entire report was prepared for the German Foreign Ministry.

[22] United States Holocaust Memorial Museum, Washington, D.C. (hereafter USHMM): 11.001M.01, 30217, "Totale Lösung der Judenfrage in Deutschland..." (no date)

[23] CZA: Z4-3567-VIII. "Auszug aus einem Rundschreiben der Zionistischen Vereinigung für Deutschland vom 20. April 1933."

[24] Bundesarchiv Berlin (hereafter BA): 15.01, Reichsministerium des Innern, 25673/28, ZVfD, Berlin, an die Auskunftsstellen des PalästinAmts, Berlin, und die Zionistischen Ortsgruppen und Vertrauensleute, 27. Okt, 1933.

[25] For more on the actions of the authorities against the ZVfD, see Hans Mommsen, "Dokumentation: Der nationalsozialistische Polizeistaat und die Judenverfolgung vor 1938," *Vierteljahrshefte für Zeitgeschichte* 10 (1962), 77-78; and Martin Rosenblüth, *Go Forth and Serve: Early Years and Public Life* (New York: Herzl Press, 1961), 247-250.

[26] CZA: S25/9703, "Confidential Report on the Zionist Situation in Germany," London, 24 March 1933. See also CZA: S25/9703, "Confidential Message from the Zionist Federation of Germany," London, 26 March 1933.

[27] See for instance CZA: S25-9703. "Confidential Report on the Zionist Situation in Germany," London, March 24, 1933; and "Confidential Message from the Zionist Federation of Germany, Brought to London on March 26, 1933.

[28] Blumenfeld, *Im Kampf*, 124 ff.

[29] See Avraham Barkai, *From Boycott to Annihilation: The Economic Struggle of German Jews, 1933-1943* (Hanover: University Press of New Rngland, 1987), chap. 2.

[30] For a complete account of the Jewish self-help efforts in

response to the disastrous economic impact of Nazi Jewish policy, see S. Adler-Rudel, *Jüdische Selbsthilfe Unter dem Naziregime 1933-1939* (Tübingen: Mohr-Siebeck, 1974). See also: Barkai, *From Boycott to Annihilation*, 39-53.

[31] CZA: S7/93, Michael Traub, z. Zt. Paris, an Martin Rosenblüth, London, 21. Oktober 1933.

[32] For a general account of the internal politics among German-Jewish organizations during the 1930s, particularly the ongoing rivalries among the Zionists, non-Zionists and anti-Zionists in the Reichsvertretung, see: Jacob Boas, "German-Jewish Internal Politics under Hitler 1933-1938," *Leo Baeck Institute Yearbook* XXIX (1984), 3-25.

[33] For the complexities of the relationship between the ZVfD and the CV during the Weimar Republic, see Paucker, *Der jüdische Abwehrkampf*, 39 ff. See also Kurt Loewenstein, "Die innerjüdische Reaktion auf die Krise der deutschen Demokratie," in Werner E. Mosse (ed.), *Entscheidungsjahr 1932*, 380-382. See also USHMM: 11.001M.31, 183 (entire file).

[34] See for example *C.V.-Zeitung*, 13. Oktober 1935.

[35] See USHMM: 11.001M.31, 183. This statement, with no author or date, refers to a recent statement in the *CV-Zeitung* of 9 May 1935 about recent "zionistische Resolutionen" regarding Zionist claims of leadership in Jewish affairs.

[36] For the history of the RjF see Ulrich Dunker, *Der Reichsbund jüdischer Frontsoldaten 1919-1938. Geschichte eines jüdischen Abwehrvereins* (Düsseldorf: Droste-Verlag, 1977).

[37] See Francis R. Nicosia, "Revisionist Zionism in Germany II: Georg Kareski and the Staatszionistische Organisation, 1933-1938," *Leo Baeck Institute Yearbook*, 32 (1987), 231-267.

[38] See for example CZA: S7/93, Zionistische Vereinigung für Deutschland an die Zionistischen Ortsgruppen und Vertrauensleute, 24. Oktober 1933.

[39] CZA: L13/138, Zionistische Vereinigung für Deutschland an die zionistischen Ortsgruppen und Vertrauensleute, 8. Februar 1934.

[40] CZA: A222/98, Robert Weltsch, Berlin, an Kurt Blumenfeld, Jerusalem, 6. Dezember 1935.

[41] CZA: S7/902, Benno Cohn, Berlin, an Georg Landauer, Jerusalem, 22. November 1938.

[42] USHMM: 11.001M.01, 4-305, Der Sicherheitsdienst der RFSS an das SD-Hauptamt, Abt. II 112, 21. Mai 1939.

[43] CZA: S5/2194, ZVfD, Berlin, an die Executive der Jewish Agency for Palestine, Jerusalem, 13. Okt. 1936.

[44] CZA: S5/432, ZVfD, Berlin an Organisations-Department der Jewish Agency for Palestine, Jerusalem, 1. Dezember 1937.

[45] CZA: S5/432, Franz Meyer, Berlin, an die Jewish Agency for Palestine, London, 29. Juli 1938.

[46] Theodor Herzl, *Der Judenstaat*, in *"Wenn Ihr wollt*, 201.

[47] CZA: S7-902, Georg Landauer/Berlin an Arthur Ruppin/ Jerusalem, 17. Februar 1939.

From Weimar to Auschwitz: Carl Schmitt and the Jurisprudence of Exclusion

Robert D. Rachlin

Introduction

The seventeenth annual Harry H. Kahn Memorial Lecture was presented on April 3, 2006, and we were honored to welcome Robert D. Rachlin from the Downs Rachlin Martin law firm of Burlington, Vermont, to the University of Vermont. He is a frequent guest on our campus, and we appreciate his interest in our German and Holocaust programs.

It is a pleasure to welcome our distinguished speaker and good friend Robert D. Rachlin from the Downs Rachlin Martin law firm right here at Burlington to the campus of the University of Vermont. As senior director of this firm, he has over forty years of experience in a wide variety of civil litigation. He has continuously been listed in *Best Lawyers in America*, and he was designated in the *2005 Chambers USA* as the only "Senior Statesman" in Vermont litigation. Among major litigation cases, he represented the State of Vermont in achieving one of the largest state court verdicts in Vermont history and has also achieved, in a trade secret misappropriation suit, the largest federal award for the state. He also represented the United States Olympic Committee in establishing U.S. license primacy over licenses granted by the International Olympic Committee. He has managed and tried many cases involving technical and scientific evidence, such as birth control litigation, cases involving mechanical engineering, and defective roofing cases. From 1961 to 1964 he was the State's Attorney of Caledonia County, Vermont.

The various legal cases have taken Robert Rachlin quite literally around the world, where his knowledge of several foreign languages (i.e., French, German, Spanish, Latin, Yiddish, and He-

brew) have served him extremely well. He has negotiated a research and development contract with a major conglomerate in
Great Britain, a license for a television series in Japan, and lease
matters connected with an international student exchange program in France; he has consulted in connection with a license for
the marketing of artistic figurines in Scotland, and he has also
dealt with clients in Finland. In addition, he has been very active
in *pro bono* representation of poor criminal defendants in Mis-
souri and Arkansas, and he has made four trips to Guantánomo,
Cuba, representing two detainees (an Algerian and a Saudi) *pro
bono*, having brought a *habeas corpus* action for them in the federal district court in Washington, D.C. In fact, Robert Rachlin received the Vermont Bar Association Distinguished Service Award
in 2003 for his work in promoting *pro bono* representation. Helping others has been a clear mission of Mr. Rachlin's approach to
legal work, as can be seen from his article on "*Pro Bono*: Searching for an Agenda" that appeared in April, 1993, in the *Vermont
Bar Journal*. Another article on "Growing Old with Judge Posner" appeared in 2003 in the same journal, dealing with Posner's
economic approach to aging.

It should also not surprise us that Mr. Rachlin has lectured to
legal groups in the United States and abroad on such topics as trial
advocacy and mediation. He is a member of the Board of Trustees
of the Vermont Law School, he has served on the Vermont Board
of Bar Examiners, he is an elected member of the American Law
Institute and an elected fellow of the American College of Trial
Lawyers and the International Society of Barristers. In addition,
he is very active in various community organizations, including
"Everybody Wins! Vermont", a school-based literacy program; he
is a concert pianist and a co-founder of the Vermont Chamber
Group, and why should he not also be a multi-engine rated pilot
and a certified flight instructor!

One might well ask how Robert Rachlin can possibly still find
the time to be the much appreciated chairperson of the Board of
Outside Advisors of the Center for Holocaust Studies here at the
University of Vermont. For more than ten years he has helped to
guide this invaluable academic program together with Prof. David
Scrase, the founding director of the UVM Holocaust Center. Together, Robert Rachlin and David Scrase have built the center into

a nationally and internationally recognized academic program within the College of Arts and Sciences at the University of Vermont. Not only has Robert Rachlin been instrumental in helping the Holocaust Center to grow so that students can now minor in Holocaust Studies, but he has also published a number of articles in the publications sponsored by this program. There is first of all his article on "How Were They Saved? Finland, the Second World War, and the Jews" that appeared in *The Bulletin of the Center for Holocaust Studies*, 3,2 (1999), 7-14. Mr. Rachlin has also published numerous book reviews in this *Bulletin*, all of them showing his erudition, his polyglot scholarship, and his broad interests in law, history, politics, and culture. Another major article on "Finland's Jews and the Final Solution" appeared in *Reflections on the Holocaust. Festschrift for Raul Hilberg on His Seventy-Fifth Birthday*, ed. by Wolfgang Mieder and David Scrase (Burlington, Vermont: The Center for Holocaust Studies at the University of Vermont, 2001), pp. 145-166; and there is also his intriguing paper on "Felix Kersten: Himmler's Doctor and the Eleventh-Hour Rescue Operations" that was published in *Making a Difference: Rescue and Assistance During the Holocaust. Essays in Honor of Marion Pritchard*, ed. by David Scrase, Wolfgang Mieder, and Katherine Quimby Johnson (Burlington, Vermont: The Center of Holocaust Studies at the University of Vermont, 2004), pp. 157-186. Other papers will surely follow as Robert Rachlin finds the time to direct his incredible energy to other Holocaust related topics.

There is no doubt that his Bachelor of Arts degree from Yale University (1957), his law degree from the University of Chicago Law School (1960), and his internationally renowned legal work during the past forty-five years have prepared him to become an adjunct professor at the University of Vermont once he retires from his law practice. I am certain that all of you will agree with me that Robert Rachlin would be a fantastic addition to the faculty of this university.

Lecture[1]

In Franz Kafka's fable *Vor dem Gesetz* (Before the Law) (1995), a man, named only as "a man from the country" comes up to the great hall of the law. The door stands open. By the door stands an imposing guard. The man from the country asks to go in but is told "no." He settles in by the guard and asks again and again to enter the hall of the law. Day after day, week after week, year after year, he is refused entry although the door remains open. He tries bribery. To no avail. Pitying him, the guard gives him a footstool, which becomes his home, as he begs in vain to enter the still open door of the hall of the law. Finally, as the man from the country is enfeebled and on the threshold of death, he asks the guard a question: "Everyone strives after the law. How is that in all these years, no one else has ever come by seeking entry?" As the man from the country draws his last breath, the guard stoops down and whispers in the ear of the withered figure: "No one else is allowed to enter. This door was meant for you alone." As the man from the country dies, the guard shuts the door.

Giorgio Agamben sees in this tale the figure of an ancient Roman institution known as *homo sacer* — which can mean either a holy man or an accursed man. *Homo sacer* was placed outside of the law. Anyone who met him might kill him, reminiscent of the mark of Cain in the book of Genesis. *Homo sacer* stood in a peculiar relationship to the law. As Agamben wrote, the law included *homo sacer* only to exclude him and excluded him only to include him — for a deadly fate (1998: 50).

The cultural and judicial environment that led to Nazi justice didn't begin with Hitler. The instability and economic crises of the Weimar Republic were fertile ground for the growth of what matured into Nazi law — a legal system that was an agent, not of equal justice, but of exclusion: exclusion of dissenters and political opponents, real or fancied; exclusion of elements deemed antisocial, including homosexuals and religious cultists; exclusion of the mentally infirm; and, of course, exclusion of non-Aryans, most particularly, the Jews.

The embryo of exclusionary judicial mind sets toward the Jews can be found in court decisions handed down years before Hitler came to power — decisions of a judiciary largely composed of holdovers from the time of Kaiser Wilhelm. Conservative, patrician judges were ill-disposed to the new-fangled republican government and its liberal institutions. An example: Weimar

Germany had a law that made it a crime to insult the established republican form of government. Decisions are recorded where attacks on the government as a *Judenrepublik* — a "Jew republic" — were overlooked on the ground that it was not the government that was really being attacked, but the Jewish influence within the country (Staff 1978: 14-22). These judges assumed that the Jews had lopsided influence in Germany and that they were a natural and appropriate target of popular anger. Judges thus veiled their anti-republican hostility to the democratic institutions of Weimar Germany by shifting their animus to history's favorite scapegoat.

The Us and Them mindset, with the Jews decisively classified among Them, was not unique to Germany. Laws proscribing Jews and limiting their ability to function economically and move about freely extended back hundreds of years. Despite the persistence of popular prejudice against Jews in Europe, even following the Enlightenment and the Napoleonic emancipation laws, the formal legal identification of Jews as Jews with the national enemy was an artifact of the National Socialist Third Reich. Similarly, the modern institutionalization of anti-Jewish animus by comprehensive, formal legislation was uniquely a feature of the Third Reich.

The deformities within Nazi law could not have developed without the theoretical groundwork laid by well-known scholars, particularly Carl Schmitt. Schmitt's theories, formed and circulated during the Weimar period, combined with growing conservative hostility to liberal institutions, which nourished a preëxisting Us and Them mentality. Strengthened by economic misery, the marriage of theory and growing anti-republicanism translated after 1933 into the Nazi legal system with its odd cohabitation of conventional legal norms and arbitrary executive decrees having the force of law. Ernst Fraenkel (1941)[2] characterized the legal system governing the Third Reich as a "dual state" (*Doppelstaat*): a state governed at once by legal norms (*Normenstaat*) and by executive measures (*Maßnahmenstaat*).

The empowerment of the executive with legislative authority, in normal times the exclusive domain of the Reichstag, was not a Nazi innovation. Article 48 of the Weimar Constitution[3] was enacted in the anticipation of a crisis situation in which the Reichstag, beset by factionalism, would be unequal to the task of providing legislation capable of meeting it. In fact, from 1919 through 1932, Article 48 was invoked more than 230 times to wrest legislative authority from the Reichstag and repose it in the Reich President (Rogers 1932). It was used not only to put down insurrection and civil disorders, but also to cope with dire economic crises. Further enhancements to executive authority were created by the Reichstag itself in the enactment in 1923 of two laws, each styled *Ermächtigungsgesetz* (enabling law), ceding to the executive the power to issue binding measures and regulations having the force of law.[4] These were precursors of the March 24, 1933 enabling law, empowering the Reich government with legislative authority along with the Reichstag.

This enactment was the key charter of the Nazi government. Its first article opens the door to the unitary powers of the executive: "Laws of the Reich may be enacted, not only by the procedures envisioned in the Reich Constitution, but also by the Reich Government."[5] The Weimar Constitution was devalued in the second article, which expressly authorized deviation from the Weimar Constitution by laws enacted by the Reich. The third article of the enabling law gave the Chancellor, Hitler, the power to issue laws for the Government. The Weimar Constitution had entrusted to the President, not the Chancellor, the initiation and proposal of laws and to the Reichstag the issuance of laws. Hitler now held that power. The constitutional allocation of that authority became moot in August 1934, when Hitler had himself named President as well as Chancellor. By these means, total legislative authority resided in Hitler. This enabling law in effect established a constitution, in which the governing norm was reducible to the will of Hitler. It enshrined the *Führerprinzip* (leader principle) as the ascendant norm of Nazi jurisprudence and the lodestar for all judges in the Third Reich. One might say that it established a constitution[6] whose guiding principle was that there is no constitution. The Weimar Constitution remained nominally in force throughout the twelve years of the Third Reich, during which the forms and formalities of legality were observed, despite deformation of the substance. The *de facto* Nazi constitutional law derived not only from the emergency powers afforded the executive by Article 48 of the Weimar Constitution, but more directly from the enabling law of March 23, 1933.

About Carl Schmitt, Gopal Balakrishnan has written that his writings "form what is arguably the most disconcerting, original and yet still unfamiliar body of twentieth-century political thought" (2000: 1). Saul Friedländer has described Schmitt as "by far the most prestigious political and legal theorist of the time" (1997: 54), that is, the years around the beginning of the Third Reich. Bernd Rüthers writes that Schmitt's role in development of legal thought in the first three years of the Third Reich was of incisive significance (*einschneidende Bedeutung*) for the legal developments that followed (2005: 100). Carl Schmitt remains today, one of the most — perhaps *the* most — challenging theoretical voice against liberalism and pluralistic parliamentary government. He has been described as "one of those figures who repel and fascinate at the same time" (Meyer).[7] His bibliography is massive,[8] but his most influential writings are a half-dozen short treatises, written before 1933, closely and rigorously reasoned. Most of these basic works have been translated into English.[9] The bulk of his writings is available only in German. This untranslated mass includes almost all of his writings during the Hitler period.

Carl Schmitt was born in 1888 in Plettenberg in the *Land* of North Rhine-Westphalia. He was raised a Roman Catholic. He received his law doctorate in 1910 and passed his law exams in 1915, a year later earning his *Habilitation*, which qualified him to teach. He served as a war volunteer with a Bavarian regiment from 1916 to 1919. After his discharge from the military following Germany's defeat in World War I, Schmitt was appointed to teach at prestigious universities, including Munich and Berlin. Shortly after the war, he published his first important treatise, *Politische Romantik* (Political Romanticism) belittling individual rights-based politics as an expression of romanticism (1919). In 1921, his *Die Diktatur* (Dictatorship) appeared, in which Schmitt distinguished between what he called commissarial dictatorship, established, as in Rome, for a limited time in order to preserve the constitutional order, and sovereign dictatorship, exercised with a view to abandoning the constitutional order and launching a new one. For Schmitt, as for Machiavelli (1962 [1531]: 202) the launch of a temporary dictatorship is sometimes essential to restore normalcy when a state is confronted with an emergency threatening its very existence.

In his 1923 *Römischer Katholizismus und politische Form* (Roman Catholicism and Political Form) Carl Schmitt styled the government of the Roman Catholic Church a *complexio oppositorum*, a complex of opposites, antinomies, contradictions (1984 [1923]: 12). The same epithet can be applied to Schmitt himself. The contradictions in his own life were remarkable. For example:

1. A Roman Catholic by upbringing (*Römischer Katholizismus* was actually printed with an ecclesiastical imprimatur) Schmitt broke with the Church when it refused him an annulment from his first marriage.

2. He was a friend, colleague, and beneficiary of Jews before the Third Reich. He wrote a letter of support that enabled Leo Strauss to study in Paris under a Rockefeller Foundation grant. Schmitt owed his first academic appointment to the Jewish economist, Moritz Julius Bonn. But he turned violently against the Jews when Hitler came to power. There is little in Schmitt's pre-Nazi writings that can be called anti-Semitic. But after Hitler came to power, he quickly cut off his correspondence with his Jewish students, colleagues and other scholars, including Strauss, and stopped answering letters from them (Meier 1988: 137).[10]

3. Schmitt's eminence as a legal scholar brought him close to the seat of government in the late Weimar Republic, where he became an important adviser to Chancellor Kurt von Schleicher and *Reichminister* Johannes von Popitz. Yet when Hitler ordered the "Night of Long Knives" against Ernst Röhm and the SA in 1934 and seized the occasion to settle other old scores, which included the murder of Schmitt's friend and patron von Schleicher and von Schleicher's wife, Schmitt a few days later wrote a fawning article in a major legal journal justifying the purges, with the jaw-dropping title *Der Führer schützt das Recht* (The Führer safeguards the law) (Schmitt 1988 [1940]: 199-203). In this article, originally published in the *Deutsche Juristen-Zeitung*,[11] Schmitt declared that the Führer, by virtue of his leadership position, was the source of law and justice. He argued that the purge of the *Sicherheitsab-*

teilung (SA) was necessary to preserve the "concrete orders,"[12] particularly in this case prevention of a merger of the army with the party.

4. As a valued counselor in the late Weimar Republic, Schmitt fought to preserve the Weimar Constitution. But after Hitler came to power, Schmitt disparaged the Weimar Constitution and publicly rejoiced in its marginalization. As a Weimar counselor, he warned publicly against both the Communists and the Nazis. But only three months after Hitler's appointment as chancellor he stood in line and formally joined the Nazi Party.

5. Before 1933, Schmitt publicly opposed the Nazis. Less than two weeks before the 1932 election, Schmitt published a newspaper article entitled *Der Mißbrauch der Legalität* (The Abuse of Legality),[13] in which he warned that anyone who allowed the Nazis to gain a majority in the election was, in his words, "acting foolishly." With the appointment of Hitler as Chancellor on January 30, 1933 and his swift consolidation of unitary power in himself and in the National Socialist Party, Schmitt's sails were quickly filled with a fresh gale. He had little trouble trimming those sails to the prevailing wind.

Schmitt's academic prestige, his vigorous literary style and the rigor of his thought opened doors to the high councils of the troubled late Weimar government. Schmitt backed a strong presidency as the only way to salvage a viable German state out of the paralysis and endless debates of contending parties and interests that bubbled in a context of a grinding economic depression, made heavier by the millstone of World War One reparations.

Schmitt's writings in the Weimar period showed a distrust of pluralistic parliamentary government, which he saw as merely a forum for debates, conflicts, interest-seeking, and position-jockeying, while the ship of state foundered. Schmitt rejected the legal positivism that had dominated German jurisprudence since the Bismarck era and was then most prominently embodied in the writings of Hans Kelsen, a Jew. For a pure positivist, there is no distinction between legality and legitimacy. In his *Legalität und Legitimität*, (Legality and Legitimacy) (1932) published in the last year of the Weimar Republic and the year that set the stage for

Hitler, Schmitt split the two concepts. He argued that legitimacy derived at bottom from popular will, whether that will was articulated in formal legislation or in measures imposed by a popular dictator. Popular sanction was the badge of democracy, even if the government it produced was totalitarian. For Schmitt as for Thomas Hobbes, the ideal state was dominated by a strong executive, ruling with the consent of the people as a whole. Amidst the turbulence of post-World War I Germany, Schmitt looked to a strengthened, authoritarian President von Hindenburg, not to the fractionalized and fractious Reichstag, for stability.

A sketch of Schmitt's pre-Third Reich political ideas can shed light on how Schmitt was able to synthesize his personal opportunism with his genuine and often profound intellectual insights. The idea most widely associated with Schmitt is the friend-enemy paradigm, set forth in what's probably his most noteworthy single book, *Der Begriff des Politischen* (The Concept of the Political) (1931). It appeared first as an essay in 1927 and was later elaborated and published as a book. Schmitt began this work by declaring that the concept of the state presupposes the concept of the political. That is, without the political, there is no state. Schmitt's *Verfassungslehre*, which was first published one year after *Der Begriff des Politischen* first appeared as an essay, makes frequent reference to the friend-enemy concept (e.g.: 214). *Begriff* can therefore be seen as conceptually anterior to *Verfassungslehre*. Without the "political," which presupposes the friend-enemy distinction, there's no need of a *Verfassungslehre*, because there is as yet no basis for creation of a state.

We recall that Hobbes derived the political from the war of each individual in the hypothetical state of nature against every other individual (*bellum omnium contra omnes*). Government was established by compact among people chiefly to protect themselves from harm, or in more modern terms, to secure the base of Abraham Maslow's hierarchy of needs: the need for physical safety. Schmitt took the war-of-all-against-all concept beyond the establishment of a social unit and proposed the existence of friends and enemies among the social units so formed. This state of enmity among social units was, for Schmitt, the necessary premise of a state.

This notion that national enmity is a fact of nature extends back to classical times. Endless war as a political institution appears in Plato's Laws. There, the Cretan oligarch, Clinias, explains the harshness of the Cretan state as shaped by the first Cretan legislator:

> *"The legislator's position would be that what most men call 'peace' is really only a fiction, and that in cold fact all states are by nature fighting an undeclared war against every other state"[14]*

For Schmitt, this natural enmity was prior to, and the presupposition of, statehood, its *raison d'être.*

Schmitt acknowledged the ambiguity of the German word for enemy (*Feind*), an ambiguity also in the English word *Enemy.* Schmitt noted that Latin and Greek distinguish between the private enemy and the public enemy. Schmitt explains that enemy in his sense is *hostis*, the public enemy, not *inimicus*, the private enemy — πολέμιος, not εχθρός. Liddell and Scott define πολέμιος as an enemy in the context of war (Liddell et al. 1996: 1432). 'Εχθρός is one who has been alienated, that is, who may once have been a friend (748). These definitions correspond to the distinction between public and private enemies. Schmitt recognized that the Christian Bible[15] enjoins its followers to "love your enemy," but he pointed out that the injunction in Latin is *diligite inimicos vestros*, not *diligite hostes vestros.* Schmitt's point is supported by the corresponding Greek text as well. The phrase is αγαπατε τους εχθρους υμων, again referring only to the private enemy, not the public enemy Schmitt had in mind. Thus, at least in this respect, Schmitt saw no clash between his friend/enemy postulate and Christian ethics.

For Schmitt the political enmity is the most extreme and intense kind. He writes: "An enemy exists only when, at least potentially, one fighting collectivity of people confronts a similar collectivity. The enemy is solely the public enemy. . . . Every concrete antagonism becomes that much more political the closer it approaches the most extreme point, that of the friend-enemy grouping" (1931: 29-30).[16]

What happens when national pugnacity or internal upheaval reaches the point of terminal instability? Who takes control in a state like Germany of 1932? Who or what is sovereign? The key for Schmitt was the *Ausnahmezustand*, the "state of exception." The state of exception is one in which extraordinary political or economic conditions call for sovereign initiatives that go beyond the established constitutional and legal order. His *Politische Theologie* (Political Theology) begins with the famous sentence: "The sovereign is he who decides on the state of exception" (*Souverän ist, wer über den Ausnahmezustand entscheidet*) (1922). Again, there were classical precedents. This concept flows from a principle reflected in Cicero's statement: *salus populi suprema lex esto*[17] (public safety must be the highest law). During the Roman Republic, temporary dictators were ordained when such a state of exception existed. Giorgio Agamben, in his *The State of Exception* (2005) sees that rubric invoked again and again throughout history and argues that it persists right up to the present day in some of the political discourse in the United States, although the term — state of exception — is not used in the current political discourse of this country.

A state of exception was foreseen by the Weimar Constitution. The suspension of normal legislative procedures and, if necessary, civil rights, by Article 48 was bound to collide with the systemic liberalism of the Weimar order and with the fundamental idea of the *Rechtsstaat*, the state governed by law. Yet, the repeated invocation of Article 48 and government by presidential decree in the final years of Weimar tended to confirm Schmitt's antagonism to liberal parliamentary democracy.

The liberalism that Schmitt opposed had among its characteristics *value neutrality* (*Wertfreiheit*) a concept associated with Max Weber, (Schmitt 2004 [1932]: 47) (Mommsen 1984: 60-62),[18] (Strauss 1965 [1953]: 40),[19] (Ciaffa 1998: 13-14). Value neutrality, in the political sense, means a theory of government in which all values have an equal chance of prevailing at a given moment in history. The state and the society are not committed *a priori* to specific values, other than what Schmitt called general liberty guarantees, that is, a certain minimal level of individual autonomy. But a value neutral state does not coerce its citizens in matters of religion, opinion, political loyalty, and the like. In this sense, the United States is a value neutral country. Saudi Arabia, for example, is not.

Schmitt attacked value neutrality, because it was inconsistent with his vision of the homogeneity that should typify a nation. If a nation, a *Volk*, is homogeneous, it follows that its people must share a common heritage and common values. For Schmitt, homogeneity is the precondition of democracy — rule by the people. For how can the people rule if they are internally at odds, one group with the other? As Schmitt's concept of the political resolves into the friend-enemy distinction, there must necessarily be a value discriminant the separates Us from Them. Raphael Gross (2000: 65) points out that "homogeneity can be seen and a political unity created only by exclusion of the heterogeneous. For Schmitt, this was the foundation of the democratic state." The friend-enemy distinction as the foundation of the political, perhaps Schmitt's most original contribution to political theory, lent itself readily to the Nazi revaluation of values which identified the Jew as the Other, the enemy. Like "godless communism" in the Cold War, or "the war on terror" in our current extraterritorial adventures, the Jew was a useful unifying symbol for all of Germany's military enemies in World War II. The Soviet Union was the enemy. But the theoretical enemy was Bolshevism. And Bolshevism was tagged as essentially Jewish. After all, Karl Marx and Leon Trotsky were Jews. The United States was the enemy. But the invisible enemy was the Jews who supposedly dominated the U.S. government, a myth that has continued traction in certain quarters today, such as the Hamas Covenant, especially the Introduction and Articles Seven, Fifteen, and Twenty.[20] No society views its mortal enemy free of values, that is, moral judgments, what my teacher Max Rheinstein called "passion-born self-deception about the enemy."[21] People do not answer uncertain calls to battle. They are not incited to act against an enemy without such value judgments.

The Nazi régime was the antithesis of a value neutral government. It was based on a foundation of four dominant values: blood, soil, party, Führer. The Nazi organization of governing values may suggest what Nietzsche (1930) called an *Umwertung aller Werte*, a revaluation or reassessment of all values. In his legal writings after the Nazi takeover, Schmitt elaborated on his identification of the Jews as the enemy. Defining and struggling against the enemy was, after all, why Schmitt contended that the state exists in the first place. Without the friend-enemy distinction at the heart of the political, the existence of the state was an anomaly.

Hitler came to power on January 30, 1933. Schmitt not only joined the Nazi Party. He offered immediate support to the first enabling law in a major law journal. He was openly pleased with the devaluation of the Reichstag. Schmitt, in effect, hailed the death of the Weimar Constitution.

Schmitt did not take long to find his anti-Semitic voice. Schmitt's friend-enemy paradigm smoothly accommodated the core values of National Socialism, particularly Blood. Blood represented likeness of kind, kinship, racial identity — *Artgleichheit* in the Nazi vocabulary. The words *Artgleichheit* and the kindred *Gleichartigkeit* (homogeneity) are not found in the German original of Schmitt's *Concept of the Political*. Nor are the words "race" and "ethnicity" to be found in the translation. But in March, 1933, Schmitt began to "update" the friend-enemy distinction. "We are learning again to make distinctions. We are learning, above all, to make the correct distinction between friend and enemy" (Schmitt 1933b). Schmitt eased himself into identifying the Jew as the Other.

It was an easy transition to the racial element, not only as a component of the friend-enemy schema, but of judicial administration. In his *Staat, Volk, Bewegung (State, People, Movement)*, (1933c: 42-46), Schmitt engaged the question that confronts judges everywhere: where does the judge look for the law when the law is undetermined? Schmitt elaborated on this idea in 1935. Writing about the Law for Amendment of the Criminal Code,[22] he argued that judges should impose penalties "according to healthy *Volk*-sensibility" (Schmitt 1935b). For the Anglo-American jurist law is determined by statute and case precedent. Where there's no precisely formulated norm, the judge probes for ethical and social value judgments beneath the surface of what has been articulated in the past. Hobbes called this "equity." For Schmitt, the source of law was to be found, not in precedent, express or implied, nor in generalized notions of equity, but in *Artgleichheit*, racial identity. The key was not the particular norm applied to the case, but the person applying it:

*"It [National Socialism] has the courage to treat the un-
equal unequally and employ the necessary differentia-
tion" (32)* [23]

If the judge was of the German race, the right result would follow
as a matter of course. When Schmitt committed himself to the
Nazi régime by joining the Party, he did not have to strain to incorporate core Nazi values into his political theory.

Schmitt's intellectual conversion from an opponent of the National Socialist Party to its enthusiastic publicist occurred with
breathtaking rapidity. Less than two weeks after enactment of the
enabling act (*Ermächtigungsgesetz*),[24] reposing effective legislative authority in the Party and the Führer, Schmitt wrote an article
praising the new law as the "provisional constitution of the German Revolution" (1933a). Less than two months after Hitler became Chancellor, Schmitt published an article in a Nazi journal
making explicit that virtually all problem areas were in one way
or another bound up with the "*Judenfrage*," the "Jewish Question"
(1933b) Race was now firmly tied to homogeneity, the linchpin
of Schmitt's accommodation to the growing mass of anti-Jewish
legislation and decrees. By 1936, Schmitt was assuring his public that "a salutary exorcism [*heilsamer Exorcismus*] would proceed from the very utterance of the word 'Jewish'" (1936:
1195f.).

When, on April 7, 1933, the Nazis enacted the so-called Law
for the accommodated himself once again, writing that "public
life must be purged of non-Aryan, alien elements" (1933b).[25] A
regulation issued under that law four days later defined "non-
Aryan" as a Jew, namely a person who had one Jewish parent or
grandparent, who was presumed to be Jewish if he or she be-
longed to the Jewish religion (*der jüdischen Religion angehört
hat*).[26] As the target of the law was unambiguously the Jews,
Schmitt's alignment with the anti-Jewish ideology of the Party
was beyond dispute.

Raul Hilberg (2003: 65) contends that the focus of Nazi anti-
Jewish legislation and decrees was religion, not physical characteristics:

*"After all, the Nazis were not interested in the 'Jewish
nose.' They were concerned with 'Jewish influence'."*

Hilberg argues (64) that Nazi commentators referred to these laws as racial laws merely for "propagandistic reasons." This view is perhaps counterintuitive, in light of the Nazi stress on *Blut* (blood) in the title of one of the Nuremberg Laws — *Gesetz zum Schutze des deutschen Blutes und der deutschen Ehre* (Law for the Protection of German Blood and German Honor)[27] — and the emphasis throughout the Nazi years on allegedly Jewish physical characteristics, always depicted as singularly repulsive.

To Schmitt these so-called Nuremberg Laws, which drastically narrowed the privileges and immunities of Jews in Germany, were not merely important laws among others, but a source of "what for us can be designated morality and public order, decency and proper behavior" (Schmitt 1935a: 1135).[28] Schmitt, the foe of value-neutrality in the law, now had a legal system rich in values derived from the racial exclusivity and anti-Semitism underlying the decrees of the régime. In a conflict between the written statutes and the spirit of these decrees there was no longer any doubt which one would prevail in the day-to-day decisions of the Nazi courts, as has been ably pointed out by Ingo Müller in his *Furchtbare Juristen* (1987) — literally, "Terrible Jurists."

The association between liberalism and Jewry was a given for Schmitt and the Nazis. Raphael Gross (2000: 119) identifies a problem created by this association. If liberalism was Jewish, how was it that so many non-Jewish German jurists advocated it? Schmitt's circular answer was that genuine German jurists were enmeshed in what he called the conceptual net (*Begriffsnetz*) of an un-German system (Schmitt 1935a: 1134). The idea of a *Rechtsstaat*, a state governed by the rule of law, was repugnant to Schmitt.[29] For him, the *Rechtsstaat* idea was one strand of the Jewish conceptual net. The *Rechtsstaat* was born of the legal positivism that Schmitt deplored. Schmitt's identification of Jews with liberalism and the *Rechtsstaat* principle (1935) lends some support to those, such as Joseph Bendersky (1983: 228),[30] who view Schmitt's anti-Semitism as purely philosophical, unconnected with the racial element. George Schwab (1989: 101) insists that Schmitt paid only "lip service to the terminology of National-Socialist propaganda." For Gross (2000: 117) the issue is moot: the bureaucracy was provided with enough definitions to make the religious and racial criteria essentially interchangeable.

The question remained: how, exactly, could one define this Jewish element in the law which Schmitt was eager to obliterate? An opportunity came on October 3rd and 4th, 1936 with a conference of legal academicians in Berlin, organized and led by Schmitt, and devoted to Jewry in Jurisprudence (*Das Judentum in der Rechtswissenschaft*) (Schmitt 1936: 1193-1199).[31] Two Nazis sufficiently distinguished to be hanged at Nuremberg, Julius Streicher and Hans Frank, sent their good wishes. Among the topics expounded at the conference: "Jewry in Economics," "Jewry in Competition Law," "Jewry in Civil Trial Law," "Jewry in Criminal Law," "Jewry and Criminality," and "The Influence of Jewish Theorists on German Public Law Theory." Schmitt gave the opening and closing lecture. In both of these addresses, Schmitt took as his text a sentence from *Mein Kampf*: "When I keep the Jew at bay, I fight for the work of the Lord" (Hitler 1934: 70).[32]

Despite his exertions, Schmitt's attempt to conceptualize the specifically Jewish in the law foundered on circularities and polemics. One example: "When we speak of Jews and Jewry, we really mean by that the Jews and no others," hardly a helpful formulation. Nor was it enough simply to equate the evil influence with what is foreign. He acknowledged that, in that case, one would have to condemn the Italian musical influence on Händel, Bach, and Mozart in the same breath as what he called the "Jewish infection that emanated from Marx or Heine." Schmitt struggled to unearth and identify the specifically Jewish in law beyond a few anti-Jewish brickbats aimed at Hans Kelsen and others. In the end Schmitt evaded definition and settled upon his own complex of opposites as a description of the Jew. This is exemplified in his closing address to the conference:

"The remarkable polarity of Jewish chaos and Jewish legalism, of anarchistic nihilism and positivistic normativism, of crude sensual materialism and abstract moralism now appears so clearly and graphically before our eyes, that we can place these facts at the foundation of our conference's decisive, scientific perception for further work in jurisprudence as well as for the science of the racial soul."

Despite his evangelical zeal to purge the law of the Jewish element and his effusive support of the régime's laws and decrees,
Schmitt found himself on the wrong end of a broadside published
by the SS in its newspaper, *Das schwarze Korps* (The Black
Corps)[33] only two months after the tangled pronouncement just
quoted was uttered. Schmitt had always been suspect to the SS
because of his pre-Third Reich association with Jews and his opposition to the Nazis during the late Weimar period. In the issue
of December 3, 1936, the paper's attack on Schmitt was oblique,
focusing on an article in *Jugendrecht*, a publication of young
lawyers, praising Schmitt for a particular contextualizing of the
Third Reich within the history of the German people over centuries. In the SS article, entitled "An Embarrassing Vindica-
tion,"[34] the unnamed author suggested that the *Jugendrecht* article
was an unwarranted attribution to Schmitt of unacceptable views
and ended by putting into Schmitt's mouth the words "Lord, save
me from my friends!"[35] By the following week, the SS writer had
"in the meantime" established that the *Jugendrecht* article wasn't
mistaken after all, that its praise of Carl Schmitt was not a misat-
tribution to Schmitt of unacceptable views. Schmitt and his views
were in fact unacceptable. The attack on Schmitt became unmistakable. Entitled, "It's Getting Even More Embarrassing,"[36] the
article recited a litany of Jews whom Schmitt had praised or from
whom he had benefited in his career. Schmitt had waited until the
last minute to cast his lot with the National Socialists. It was only
then that Schmitt saw the light and became an anti-Semite, quiet-
ly expunging citations of Jewish authors from his published
works. Fortunately for Schmitt's physical survival, he had powerful friends in Hans Frank and Hermann Goering, but he lost almost all of his official positions as a result of the SS denunciation.
He was able to retain a professorship in Berlin, however. Thereafter, stripped of his credibility with the ruling powers, Schmitt
confined his writings to issues that did not directly touch on the
form of national government and its policies.

The denunciation by the SS may have saved Schmitt serious
consequences after the war, when Schmitt was interned for two
years, held for a possible trial at Nuremberg, which in fact never
happened. He was interrogated on suspicion of providing intellectual support to Hitler's aggressive war and of even having been

a collaborator in plans for the war. This interrogation, and
Schmitt's oral and written responses, are preserved in a book entitled *Antworten in Nürnberg* (Answers in Nuremberg) (Schmitt,
Quaritsch, and Kempner 2000). Schmitt again and again referred
to what he called the *Diffamierung* (defamation) by the SS as
proof of how far removed he was from the atrocities of the Nazi
régime, palpably a *non sequitur*.

In the end, he was released, and he returned to his old home
at Plettenberg, where he wrote about what he called the *Nomos* of
the earth, the ordering of the planet's land and resources (1950).
For Schmitt, the organization of the earth after World War II was
based, no longer on sovereignty over land, but on economics and
production capacity. He compared the modern world *Nomos* to a
beehive, a strangely Marxist analogy.

Between his release and his death in 1985, international interest in Schmitt mushroomed. His home became a shrine, not only
for right-wing nationalists, but for serious scholars. A flood of
ink has flowed, and still flows, about Schmitt in books and
learned journals. The journal *Telos*, in particular, has devoted
much space to articles about him. This shows a vigorous interest
in what was of value in Schmitt's thought. Schmitt, in his pre-
Nazi writings, challenged conventional Western assumptions
about liberal parliamentary democracy, the presuppositions of a
viable nation-state, and the notion of the rule of law. He was the
first modern German jurist to break sharply with the prevailing
positivism, embracing a plebiscitary theory of legitimacy whose
roots can be traced back to Periclean Athens. He challenged our
conventional identification of democracy with liberal representative government. Like Hobbes and Machiavelli, he forced his
readers to confront human nature at its darkest, in fact celebrated
it as the keystone of the state, by proposing what can be described
as a predatory disposition toward enemies as the condition *sine
qua non* of statehood.

But why study Schmitt at all? After all, he was a card-carry-
ing Nazi. Like Martin Heidegger, he lent his name and fame to a
clique of crude men bent on annihilating whole civilizations and
cultures. Leo Strauss, in his *Natural Right and History* (1965
[1953]: 42-43), remarked that we should beware of the logical fallacy that he called the *reductio ad Hitlerum*, noting that "a view

is not refuted by the fact that it happens to have been shared by Hitler." The same principle applies to views held by those who supported or empowered Hitler. To be sure, viewed objectively and without indulgence of the *reductio ad Hitlerum*, we can safely dismiss most of what Schmitt penned between 1933 and 1936 as of historical interest only. The scholarly rigor present in Schmitt's pre-Hitler writings is palpably absent in most of his writings during these years. The kernel of his serious thought is another matter.

Schmitt challenges us to confront uncomfortable questions about the future of the kind of government that we, especially in the West, have come to view as axiomatic — indeed worthy of export abroad willy-nilly to peoples and cultures adhering to very different ideas about how they should be governed. His friend-enemy concept has a contemporary resonance. There have been few if any intervals in the last hundred years in which the United States did not have an enemy, defined by national boundaries, by ideology, or both. Yet we know of many countries that seem to function nicely without what Schmitt would call an enemy. But is Schmitt's friend-enemy paradigm at least a partial truth? Is it awakened by contingencies of time and circumstances? Does our own democracy consistently reflect the popular will? Is it, indeed, a democracy in any sense that Plato or Aristotle would credit, let alone Schmitt? Does the partisan wrangling in our Congress suggest the kind of shifting and compromising that Schmitt saw as beneath the demise of the Weimar Republic in a time of crisis? Is the United States now in an *Ausnahmezustand*, a state of exception, in which government may or must set aside established legal norms to ensure the *salus populi*, the public safety?[37]

The pre- and post-Nazi Schmitt is worth study as we examine our accepted political postulates and as an ingredient of our national debate about the future of liberal democratic institutions in the face of ideological, terrorist, and environmental challenges to our survival. We may reject most of what Schmitt taught. But if so, we must so do on the merits, not out of hand because of Schmitt's unsavory personal history or the *reductio ad Hitlerum*.

Is Schmitt fairly included among those to blame for the Holocaust? There is no reason to believe that Schmitt advocated the physical extermination of the Jews, that he supported the Final

Solution, or even knew much if anything about it at the time. In his post-war writings and his interrogations as a prisoner, he claimed to be shocked by it. Nevertheless, he gave significant moral aid to the régime by lending his name and prestige to the exclusion of the Jews from the protections of the law and to their demonization as the implacable Other, and he calibrated his theoretical position to the imperatives of the National Socialist scheme of government, all without an appearance of effort or embarrassment.

Carl Schmitt has been called the *Kronjurist* (the Crown Jurist) of the Third Reich. By deploying his friend-enemy paradigm to serve the Nazi de-legitimation of the Jews and denial of the protections that a civilized society extends to all of its inhabitants, Schmitt helped to convert the Jew into *homo sacer*, the accursed man. The law included him only to exclude him, and excluded him only to include him for *Sonderbehandlung*, special treatment. Whatever Carl Schmitt did or did not know about Auschwitz, Baba Yar, Treblinka, and Drancy, he cannot be exonerated as a mere footnote to the jurisprudence of exclusion. Joseph Bendersky has emphasized the absence of anti-Semitism in his pre-Third Reich writings and personal relationships (1983: 137). He writes that "there was not the slightest anti-Semitic note in any of his writings of personal relationships" and points out the Schmitt dedicated his *Verfassungslehre* to Dr. Fritz Eisler, a Jewish classmate who fell in World War I (227). Paul Gottfried (1990, 39) claims that, in his later years, Schmitt actually hallucinated about Eisler. Andreas Göbel, et al. (1995: 80, note 27) mention a rumor that Eisler had secretly co-authored an early work with Schmitt. Bendersky[38] writes that after the anti-Jewish boycott in the spring of 1933, Schmitt's wife visited the Eisler home in Hamburg as Schmitt himself tried to comfort them by telephone.

Whatever his personal views about the Jews, as distinct from what he may have written to secure his position in the Nazi régime, he lent his powerful name and reputation to the legitimation of a murderous political enterprise. He was a key component of what Julien Benda, in another context, called "la trahison des clercs" (1965 [1927]), the betrayal of the intellectuals. Max Weinreich (1946) devoted a book to the participation of jurists, historians, philosophers, and scholars generally in lending prestige to the new order. Martin Heidegger is the best known philosopher enthusiastically underwriting the Nazi régime. Composers, such as Richard Strauss, Carl Orff, and Hans Pfitzner must be added to this list.[39] Many of these luminaries, while publishing ideas and creating works of lasting value, sought personal advancement by allowing themselves to be used by a clique of odious rulers with whom, in private life, they would likely have disdained to break bread.

As in the Kafka fable, the door to the law stood open for the Jew only to keep him out. Unlike in the Kafka fable, the door did let him in at the last moment, but only to shut him out of the chamber itself and shunt him off to a chamber of a very different sort. Schmitt, like his intellectual fellow travelers — whatever the depth of their personal convictions — cannot evade their share of responsibility for the horrors that they helped enable through their intellectual trahison.

Notes:
[1] Robert D. Rachlin is Senior Director, Downs Rachlin Martin PLLC, Burlington, Vermont; Chair, Advisory Board, Carolyn and Leonard Miller Center for Holocaust Studies, University of Vermont; Adjunct Lecturer, Department of German and Russian, University of Vermont; Distinguished Lecturer, Vermont Law School. All translations are the author's unless otherwise indicated.

[2] This work, originally written and published in English, was many years later translated into the Fraenkel's native German. (Fraenkel, Ernst, and Alexander von Brünneck. 2001. *Der Doppelstaat.* Hamburg: Europaïsche Verlagsanstalt.)

[3] "In case public safety is seriously threatened or disturbed, the Reich President may take the measures necessary to reestablish law and order, if necessary using armed force. In the pursuit of this aim, he may suspend the civil rights described in articles 114, 115, 117, 118, 123, 124 and 153, partially or entirely."

(*"Reichspräsident kann, wenn im Deutschen Reiche die öffentliche Sicherheit und Ordnung erheblich gestört oder gefährdet wird, die zur Wiederherstellung der öffentlichen Sicherheit und Ordnung nötigen Maßnahmen treffen, erforderlichenfalls mit Hilfe der bewaffneten Macht einschreiten. Zu diesem Zwecke darf er vorü bergehend die in den Artikeln 114, 115, 117, 118, 123,*

124 und 153 festgesetzten Grundrechte ganz oder zum Teil außer Kraft setzen.") The cited articles protected, among other fundamental civil rights, the inviolability of the home, the privacy of correspondence, freedom of speech, and freedom from arbitrary detention.

[4] *Reichsgeseztblatt* (1923), I., 943, 1179.

[5] *"Reichsgesetze können außer in dem in der Reichsverfassung vorgesehenen Verfahren auch durch die Reichsregierung beschlossen werden."*

[6] "Constitution" is used in the broad, vernacular sense of a document embodying an overall legal framework for the organization and functioning the state. Carl Schmitt carefully distinguished multiple senses of the word "constitution" (*Verfassung*). I use the term in what Schmitt would call the "relative concept of the constitution" (*relativer Verfassungsbegriff*), which can include the written document, "constitutional law" (*Verfassungsgesetz*) in Schmitt's usage. For Schmitt, "constitution" in the absolute sense (*absoluter Verfassungsbegriff*) is not a document or a set of legal norms, but an act of political will by the people to incorporate themselves as a state (Schmitt 1993 [1928]: 1-20).

[7] *"Carl Schmitt gehört zu jenen Gestalten, die gleichzeitig abstoßen und faszinieren."*

[8] The Flemish scholar Piet Tommissen attempted over several years to construct a bibliography. An early effort (1953) is modestly, perhaps realistically, entitled *Versuch* (effort, attempt). Raphael Gross (2000: 7) relates further efforts by Tommissen in 1959, 1968, and 1978, noting that these contain over 1,600 entries. The *Versuch* lists 412 works by or about Schmitt, including translations. Whatever that number would be today, there's no doubt that it is vastly greater than in 1953. I have been unable personally to examine Tommissen's Schmitt bibliographies, other than the 1953 *Versuch*.

[9] The most complete bibliography of English-translated books and articles by Schmitt that I have been able to find is available at http://www.theoria.ca/research/files/SchmittEnglish.pdf (last visited July 18, 2008). It purports to be complete as of August 23, 2007.

[10] Joseph Bendersky contends that Schmitt's cessation of correspondence with Jews was not total. "Schmitt apparently distin-

guished between those he would help and those whose letters he left unanswered." Joseph Bendersky, "New Evidence, Old Contradictions: Carl Schmitt and the Jewish Question," *Telos* 2005 (Fall 2005): 64-82, 69. Bendersky claims that "in the first months of the Third Reich, Schmitt worried about the fate of his Jewish friends and colleagues. . . ." Bendersky offers no substantiation of this statement, at least in the cited article.

[11] August 1, 1934, 945-950.

[12] The "orders" (*Stände*) would comprise, among others, the family, churches, army, and state bureaucracy. Schmitt expanded on the juristic role of the *Stände* in a full chapter of his *Über die drei Arten des rechtswissenschaftlichen Denkens* (1934).

[13] *Tägliche Rundschau*, July 19, 1932.

[14] Bk. I, 626a, trans. Trevor J. Saunders in *Plato: Complete Works* (Indianapolis: Hackett, 1997), 1320.

[15] Matthew 5:44.

[16] The translation is that of George Schwab in Carl Schmitt, *The Concept of the Political*. (Chicago: University of Chicago Press, 2007), 28-29.

[17] De legibus, III. iii. 8.

[18] The cited work is a translation of the original, i.e., (Mommsen 1959).

[19] See, also, "Weber, Max" *Dictionary of the Social Sciences*. Craig Calhoun, ed. Oxford University Press 2002. "Value-neutrality" can be defined as "the expectation . . . that scientists will (or at least should) eliminate all biases and preferences at each stage of their studies." John Scott and Gordon Marshall, *A Dictionary of Sociology*. Oxford University Press 2005. *Oxford Reference Online*. Oxford University Press. University of Vermont. 20 August 2008 http://www.oxfordreference.com/views/ENTRY.html?subview=Main&entry=t88.e2444 (last accessed August 20, 2008).

[20] The text of the Covenant in English can be found at http://www.yale.edu/lawweb/avalon/mideast/hamas.htm (last accessed August 11, 2008).

[21] Review of Ferdinand A. Hermens, *Tyrants' War and Peoples' Peace* (Chicago: University of Chicago Press), *The University of Chicago Law Review*, 12:104-107. December, 1944.

[22] "*Gesetz zur Änderung des Strafgesetzbuches.*" Reichsgesetzblatt (1935), I., 839.

[23] "*Er [der Nationalsozialismus] hat den Mut Ungleiches ungleich zu behandeln und notwendige Differenzierungen durchzusetzen.*"

[24] *Reichsgesetzblatt* (1933), I., 141.

[25] "*[D]as öffentiliche Leben von nichtarischen fremdgearteten Elementen ... reinigen [solle].*"

[26] "*Erste Verordnung zur Durchführung des Gesetzes zur Wiederherstellung des Berufsbeamtentums.*" *Reichsgesetzblatt* (1933), I., 195. In a regulation of November 14, 1935 supplementing the Nuremberg Laws, the term *Religionsgemeinschaft* (religious community) is substituted for *Religion. Reichsgesetzblatt* (1935), I., 1333.

[27] *Reichsgesetzblatt* (1935), I., 1146-1147.

[28] "*. . . was für uns Sittlichkeit und öffentliche Ordnung, Anstand und gute Sitten genannt werden [könne].*"

[29] This repugnance was not at all evident in his *Verfassungslehre* (1993 [1928], a magisterial treatment of constitutional theory. The second of four parts of the work is entitled "The *Rechtsstaat* Component of the Modern Constitution" (*Der rechtsstaatliche Bestandteil der modernen Verfassung*).

[30] "[H]e found himself articulating ideas about race and the Jews, which he thought were truly absurd."

[31] I am indebted to Professor Geri Solomon, Assistant Dean and Curator of Special Collections at Hofstra University, who was kind enough to photocopy pertinent sections of the original German published account of this 1936 conference for me. The cited text is also available at the Library of Congress, Law Library Reading Room (Madison, LM201).

[32] "*Indem ich mich des Juden erwehre, kämpfe ich für das Werk des Herrn.*"

[33] December 3, 1936, "Eine peinliche Ehrenrettung," 14; December 10, 1936, "Es wird immer noch pienlicher," 2. This periodical is available on microfilm at the New York Public Library, Main Building, Room 100.

[34] "*Eine peinliche Ehrenrettung.*"

[35] "*Herr, rette mich vor meinen Freunden!*" (exclamation point in original).

[36] "*Es wird immer noch peinlicher!*" (exclamation point in original).

[37] Agamben (2005) argues that the United States has been in a continuous state of exception since World War II. It is doubtful that Schmitt would agree, given the intensity of the crisis that informs what he termed the *Ausnahmezustand.*

[38] Joseph Bendersky, *op. cit.* note 11, 68.

[39] Michael Kater (2002) has documented the role of composers.

Works Cited:

Agamben, Giorgio. 1998. *Homo sacer: sovereign power and bare life.* Stanford, Calif.: Stanford University Press.

—. 2005. *State of Exception.* Translated by K. Attell. Chicago and London: University of Chicago Press.

Balakrishnan, Gopal, and Carl Schmitt. 2000. *The enemy: an intellectual portrait of Carl Schmitt.* London; New York: Verso.

Benda, Julien. 1965 [1927]. *La trahison des clercs.* Utrecht: J. J. Pauvert.

Bendersky, Joseph W. 1983. *Carl Schmitt, theorist for the Reich.* Princeton, N.J.: Princeton University Press.

Ciaffa, Jay A. 1998. *Max Weber and the Problems of Value Free Social Science.* Lewisburg: Bucknell University Presses.

Fraenkel, Ernst. 1941. *The dual state: a contribution to the theory of dictatorship.* New York, London: Oxford University Press.

Friedländer, Saul. 1997. *Nazi Germany and the Jews.* 1st ed. 2 vols. Vol. 1, The years of persecution, 1933-1939. New York: HarperCollins.

Göbel, Andreas, Dirk van Laak, and Ingeborg Villinger. 1995. *Metamorphosen des Politischen: Grundfragen politischer Einheitsbildung seit den 20er Jahren.* Berlin: Akademie Verlag.

Gottfried, Paul. 1990. *Carl Schmitt: politics and theory, Contributions in political science, no. 264.* New York: Greenwood Press.

Gross, Raphael. 2000. *Carl Schmitt und die Juden: eine deutsche Rechtslehre.* 1. Aufl. ed. Frankfurt am Main: Suhrkamp.

Hilberg, Raul. 2003. *The destruction of the European Jews.* 3rd ed. New Haven, Conn.: Yale University Press.

Hitler, Adolf. 1934. *Mein Kampf.* Munich: Franz Eher.

Kafka, Franz. 1995. *Meistererzählungen.* Zürich: Diogenes.

Kater, Michael H. 2002. *Composers of the Nazi era: eight portraits*. New York: Oxford University Press.

Liddell, Henry George, Robert Scott, Henry Stuart Jones, and Roderick McKenzie. 1996. *A Greek-English lexicon*. Rev. and augm. throughout / ed. Oxford: Clarendon Press; New York: Oxford University Press.

Machiavelli, Niccolò. 1962 [1531]. *The Prince and the Discourses*. New York: Carlton House.

Meier, Heinrich. 1988. *Carl Schmitt, Leo Strauss und "Der Begriff des Politischen": Dialog unter Abwesenden*. Stuttgart: J. B. Metzler.

Meyer, Thomas. 2002. Eine Studie von Raphael Gross: "Carl Schmitt und die Juden". Review of Reviewed Item. *hagalil.com*, http://www.hagalil.com/archiv/2000/12/schmitt. htm.

Mommsen, Wolfgang J. 1959. *Max Weber und die deutsche Politik, 1890-1920*. Tübingen: Mohr.

—-. 1984. *Max Weber and German politics, 1890-1920*. Chicago: University of Chicago Press.

Müller, Ingo. 1987. *Furchtbare Juristen: die unbewältigte Vergangenheit unserer Justiz*. München: Kindler.

Nietzsche, Friedrich. 1930. *Der Wille zur Macht, Versuch einer Umwertung aller Werte*. Leipzig: A. Kröner.

Rogers, Lindsay, et al. 1932. German Political Institutions, II. Article 48. *Political Science Quarterly* 47:583-594.

Rüthers, Bernd. 2005. *Die unbegrenzte Auslegung: zum Wandel der Privatrechtsordnung im Nationalsozialismus*. Tübingen: Mohr-Siebeck.

Schmitt, Carl. 1919. *Politische Romantik*. Munich: Duncker & Humblot.

—-. 1922. *Politische Theologie: Vier Kapitel zur Lehre von der Souveränität*. Munich: Duncker & Humblot.

—-. 1931. *Der Begriff des Politischen*. Hamburg: Hanseatische Verlagsanstalt.

—-. 1932. *Legalität und Legitimität*. Munich: Duncker & Humblot.

—-. 1933a. Das Gesetz zur Behebung der Not von Volk und Reich. *Deutsche Juristen-Zeitung* 38 (7):455-458.

—-. 1933b. Das gute Recht der deutschen Revolution. *Westdeutscher Beobachter, Amtliches Organ der NSDAP*.

—. 1933c. *Staat, Bewegung, Volk; die Dreigliederung der politischen Einheit.* Hamburg,: Hanseatische Verlagsanstalt.

—. 1934. *Über die drei Arten des rechtswissenschaftlichen Denkens.* Hamburg: Hanseatische Verlagsanstalt.

—. 1935a. Die Verfassung der Freiheit. *Deutsche Juristen-Zeitung* 40 (19):1133-1155.

—. 1935b. Kodifikation oder Novelle? Über die Aufgabe und Methode der heutigen Gesetzgebung. *Deutsche Juristen-Zeitung* 40:919-925.

—. 1936. "Das Judentum in der deutschen Rechtswissenschaft" in "Die deutsche Rechtswissenschaft im Kampf gegen den jüdischen Geist". *Deutsche Juristen-Zeitung* 41 (20):1193-1199.

—. 1950. *Der Nomos der Erde im Völkerrecht des Jus publicum Europaeum.* Köln,: Greven.

—. 1984 [1923]. *Römischer Katholizismus und politische Form.* Stuttgart: Klett-Cotta.

—. 1988 [1940]. *Positionen und Begriffe in Kampf mit Weimar - Genf - Versailles, 1923-1939.* Berlin: Duncker & Humblot.

—. 1993 [1928]. *Verfassungslehre.* 8. Aufl. ed. Berlin: Duncker & Humblot.

—. 2004 [1932]. *Legality and Legitimacy.* Translated by J. Setzer. Durham and London: Duke University Press.

Schmitt, Carl, Helmut Quaritsch, and Robert M. W. Kempner. 2000. *Carl Schmitt: Antworten in Nürnberg.* Berlin: Duncker & Humblot.

Schwab, George. 1989. *The challenge of the exception: an introduction to the political ideas of Carl Schmitt between 1921 and 1936.* 2nd ed, *Contributions in political science, no. 248.* New York: Greenwood Press.

Staff, Ilse. 1978. *Justiz im Dritten Reich: eine Dokumentation.* Orig. Ausg., [2. Aufl.] ed. Frankfurt am Main: S. Fischer-Taschenbuch-Verlag.

Strauss, Leo. 1965 [1953]. *Natural Right and History.* Chicago: University of Chicago Press.

Tommissen, Piet. 1953. *Versuch einer Carl-Schmitt Bibliographie.* Düsseldorf: Academia Moralis.

Weinreich, Max. 1946. *Hitler's Professors, YIVO English Translation Series.* New York: Yiddish Scientific Institute.

Franklin D. Roosevelt and the American Response to the Holocaust: An Historiographical Controversy

Mark Stoler

Introduction

The eighteenth annual Harry H. Kahn Memorial Lecture was presented on March 26, 2007, and we were honored to have our very own Prof. Mark Stoler from the Department of History at the University of Vermont as our distinguished speaker. He has been a personal friend of the Kahn family for four decades, and we appreciate his long interest in our Department of German and Russian and the Center for Holocaust Studies.

As I begin my introduction of our well-known and acclaimed colleague and friend Prof. Mark Stoler from the Department of History here at the University of Vermont, let me first mention that Prof. Stoler has been a dear friend of the Kahn family for many years, and I know that they are extremely pleased to have one of Prof. Kahn's best friends present this lecture in his honor. I am also certain that Prof. Kahn would be overjoyed to have his erudite friend give this very presentation as one of his last public addresses before his retirement at the end of this academic year after almost forty years of loyal service to the University of Vermont. Of course, Prof. Stoler is really not retiring in the normal sense of that word. Next year he will be the Stanley Kaplan Visiting Professor in American Foreign Policy at Williams College, and surely there will be other such opportunities here and abroad. There will also be more books forthcoming from his ever active mind searching for deeper insights into the perplexities of human history.

Prof. Stoler earned his B.A. degree from City College of New York in 1966, receiving his M.A. degree one year later from the

University of Wisconsin at Madison. In 1970 he arrived on the UVM campus, completing his Ph.D. in 1971 at the University of Wisconsin with a specialization in Twentieth Century U.S. Diplomatic & Military History. Prof. Stoler's field of study reminds me of what Franklin D. Roosevelt once observed to his war-time friend Winston S. Churchill: "It is fun to be in the same decade with you." We, who have worked with Mark Stoler for several decades, and his hundreds of students would certainly want to echo these words as we have learned and benefitted from his vast knowledge and friendship.

A glance at Prof. Stoler's curriculum vitae quickly reveals his incredible scholarly energy and prolific output of seminal books most of which I have with kind inscriptions on my bookshelves at home. There is his early study on *The Politics of the Second Front: American Military Planning and Diplomacy in Coalition Warfare, 1941-1943* (1977), followed by *The Origins of the Cold War* (1982), and his invaluable study on *George C. Marshall: Soldier-Statesman of the American Century* (1989). His detailed investigation of *Allies and Adversaries: The Joint Chiefs of Staff, the Grand Alliance, and U.S. Strategy in World War II* (2000) received the Distinguished Book Award for the Society for Military Studies, and his two most recent books are *Debating Franklin D. Roosevelt's Foreign Policies, 1933-1945* (2005, co-authored with Justus Doenecke) and *Allies in War: Britain and America Against the Axis, 1940-1945* (2005).

His various book chapters, his papers published in conference proceedings, and his articles that have appeared in some of the leading journals in North America, Europe, and the Near East are too numerous to mention, but here are a few titles at least that will indicate how far and wide Prof. Stoler casts his scholarly net: "The Pacific-First Alternative in American World War II Strategy" (1980), "The Mission Concept and the Role of Ideology in American Foreign Policy: A Historical Assessment" (1987), "The Soviet Union and the Second Front in American Strategic Planning, 1941-1942" (1989), "Dwigth D. Eisenhower: Architect of Victory" 1994), "The United States: The Global Strategy" (1994), "The `Wise Owl': George D. Aiken and Foreign Affairs, 1941-1975" (1995), "The Second World War in American History and Memory" (2000), "World War II Diplomacy" (2003), and "War and

Diplomacy: or, Clausewitz for Diplomatic Historians" (2005). His research has been supported by numerous prestigious grants from such agencies as the Ford Foundation, the National Endowment of the Humanities, and the American Philosophical Society, with two Fulbright fellowships giving him the opportunity of spending extended periods of time in Israel. In addition, he has held several guest professorships at the United States Naval War College, the United States Military Academy, and the United Sates Army Military History Institute. All of this published work also informs Prof. Stoler's magisterial and legendary teaching abilities. In fact, he has also written textbooks for his eager students. There is the two-volume set of *Explorations in American History: A Skills Approach* (1980), co-authored with his UVM colleague Marshall True and, more recently, the book on *Major Problems in the History of World War II* (2003), this time co-authored with his UVM colleague Melanie Gustafson. There is no doubt that Prof. Stoler has worked untiringly for his many students, and in turn fascinating, exciting, and yes inspiring them to do ever better historical work. The list of courses and seminars that he has taught during more than three decades illustrates how his mind has always looked for new challenges, as for example: United States Military History, History of the Second World War, History of American Radicalism, Origin of the Cold War, Foreign Policies of the Founding Fathers, Political and Religious Thought of Reinhold Niebuhr, The Era of Franklin D. Roosevelt, etc. For all of these efforts he was awarded the Kroepsch Maurice Award for Excellence in Teaching in the category of full professor in 2006. Of course, he had already received the College of Arts and Sciences Deans's Lecture Award for Outstanding Scholarship and Teaching in 1992 and the University Scholar Award in 1993. Even earlier, in 1984, he was honored with UVM's most coveted George V. Kidder Outstanding Faculty Award. Having received the four most distinguished awards that the University of Vermont can bestow upon a faculty member, Prof. Stoler can indeed look back at his influential and productive career with much pride and satisfaction, and we can applaud and commend him for his many years of serving the University of Vermont as scholar, teacher, mentor, and friend.

Lecture

I am deeply honored by Professor Wolfgang Mieder's invitation to deliver this lecture—and very touched personally. Harry Kahn was one of the first senior faculty members to befriend me when I arrived at UVM thirty seven years ago, and the first to ask me to give a public lecture—at the Hillel House then on College Street. It is thus quite fitting that I give one of my last public lectures at UVM in his honor. That this is the eighteenth annual Kahn lecture only adds to the honor, for the Hebrew word for eighteen, "Chai," has special significance in that it also spells out the word "life."

My relationship with Harry did not end after that first lecture-despite the fact that the lecture did not exactly contain what Harry or his audience had wanted to hear, and that a huge cultural and "generation gap" clearly separated us. Nevertheless, I soon developed a close relationship with Harry and his family. He arranged for my first trip to Israel, out of which eventually emerged both my Fulbright Professorship at the University of Haifa and two of my closest and dearest friendships: with Professor Frank Manchel and Rabbi Max Wall. I was also a frequent guest in the Kahn home, and in 1979 I became the recipient of a gift that I greatly treasured for many years: Harry's and Irene's 1947 extra refrigerator, which I used for many years in my summer camp in Starksboro. Despite its age it functioned very well, save for a defective door in the small freezer section. When I asked Irene why she had not simply replaced that door and kept the refrigerator, she told me that the repairman had said to her "Lady, this refrigerator is older than I am!" I remember that line well because the same now holds for me vis-à-vis my own appliances!

The Kahn lectures are supposed to deal with German and/or Jewish history. These are not my fields of historical study. But within the history of U.S. foreign relations which is my specialty, there is a relevant topic: Franklin D. Roosevelt and the American response to the Holocaust. It is also a major and controversial issue in my field, one that has inspired a very large literature filled with disagreements. Indeed, in preparing the World War II diplomacy chapter for a new annotated bibliography in the history of U.S. foreign relations, this became one of my largest and most controversial sections.[1]

What I intend to do today is give you the history of that literature and those interpretive disagreements. Such an analysis is known in my field as historiography, the history of the writing of history. And as you will see, it is far different from an analysis of the event itself. The historiography on this particular subject differs from the standard historiographical pattern in the history of U.S. foreign relations. Within that field, the standard pattern is the appearance first of the official interpretation as enunciated by the president and/or the secretary of state and supported by the first generation of journalists and historians, followed by a revisionist interpretation that sharply challenges the official interpretation, and then an attempted synthesis. Typical in this regard is the historiography of the decision to drop the atomic bomb on Japan in 1945. Early interpretations echoed President Harry S Truman's claim that the key factor in the decision had been the desire to end the war as quickly as possible and with the lowest cost in life. During the 1960s, however, revisionist historians argued that the primary motive had been a desire to cow the Soviet Union and minimize its postwar power, and that this had constituted a reversal of Roosevelt's pro-Soviet policies by his successor. By the 1970s a new generation of historians had come up with a synthesis by arguing that the two motives were complementary rather than contradictory, and that the anti-Soviet component had actually been initiated by Roosevelt rather than Truman.[2]

This standard pattern does not hold for Roosevelt and the American response to the Holocaust. Instead of a first generation defending U.S. behavior, we have total silence on the issue for more than twenty years, followed by a host of sharply critical scholars and then by revisionists who ironically defend Roosevelt against many of the charges leveled by the previous critics. What I would like to do here today is explain and explore this different pattern in some detail, and in the process try to offer some reasons as to why it has developed on this particular issue.

From 1945 to 1967 the U.S. response to the Holocaust was essentially a non-topic in the history of U.S. foreign relations. When the issue was on occasion raised, the standard approach was that no one knew what was happening before the death camps were liberated in 1945 and that nothing could have been done to stop the slaughter even if the facts had been known save to win the war as quickly as possible—which was exactly what we did. But what was most notable prior to 1968 was the almost total silence on the issue. No full-length works were published on the subject. Indeed, the diplomatic history textbooks I read as an undergraduate and graduate student did not even mention it. For all intents and purposes, it was a non-issue.

Partially this resulted from the fact that most of the key U.S. and British World War II documents remained classified until the 1960s and 1970s. But that fact did not preclude the historical examination of numerous other wartime issues between 1945 and 1967. More was involved in the twenty-two-year silence on this particular issue.

A key related factor was the near-total silence on the Holocaust itself. As Michael Neufeld has recently noted, "It is difficult to imagine now to what extent the Holocaust . . . was peripheral to the public memory of World War II before the 1960s."[3] The same held true for scholars; Raul Hilberg has pointedly noted in this regard that his doctoral adviser at Columbia University in the early 1950s, warned him that a focus on this topic would be doom his career.[4]

There were numerous reasons for such silence. The war itself and the ensuing Cold War—not the Holocaust—were the key issues for two decades after the war. Furthermore, victimhood was not popular in American culture during this time period. Nor was uniqueness. And anti-Semitism was still a potent force in the United States during this time. So was a desire for assimilation by American Jews. Consequently neither they nor anyone else wished to dwell on the issue. Shock may have also played a role; it simply took time for an event of such magnitude and unbelievability to sink in.

The first major studies of the U.S. response to the Holocaust were published in 1967-68: Arthur Morse's *While Six Million Died* and David Wyman's *Paper Walls*, which covered the years 1938-1941. Both were highly critical of Roosevelt and the State Department, and Morse's book became a best seller whose findings shocked many of its readers (I still remember in that regard my father's combination of disbelief and rage as he read the volume). Major additional attacks then followed throughout the

1970s and reached floodtide in the early 1980s, with titles and subtitles often revealing of their highly critical theses: *A Chronicle of Apathy; the Politics of Rescue; No Haven for the Oppressed; The Failure of Rescue; The Terrible Secret; The Jews Were Expendable; Were We Our Brothers' Keepers?; The Deafening Silence; The Holocaust Conspiracy.*[5] Most comprehensive, and devastating, was David Wyman's 1984 volume, *The Abandonment of the Jews,* which in turn became the basis for the 1994 PBS television special "America and the Holocaust: Deceit and Indifference" and charged the United States with being the "passive accomplices" of the Nazis.[6]

These works made clear that the U.S. government, press and people clearly did know about Nazi persecution of German Jews during the 1930s, but nevertheless refused to allow most of them into the United States as refugees. That policy did not change after the war began in 1939, or after U.S. entry in late 1941. By late 1942 the U.S. Government also knew about the genocide underway and the existence of the death camps but did nothing. Those camps, many critics argued, both could and should have been bombed, but the armed forces refused to do so and the administration refused to order them to do so. News of the death camps was also available to the American people as a whole, who also did nothing. This record of inaction, these early scholars concluded, constitutes one of the worst blots on Franklin Roosevelt's record. Roosevelt biographer Robert Dallek seconded that judgment in a major 1979 work that ironically defended FDR against earlier criticisms while leveling this new criticism.[7]

According to the critics, numerous factors accounted for American inaction and insensitivity. The base was a pre-existing nativism, with anti-immigrant legislation that established exceptionally low quotas for East Europeans dating back to the 1920s. Such anti-immigrant sentiments were only reinforced by the Great Depression of the 1930s, for immigrants were perceived as constituting competition for scarce jobs; consequently nearly 80 percent of Americans polled in the 1930s opposed any revision of the immigration quotas. Another key factor was pre-existing anti-Semitism, both by the American people as a whole and by specific government officials in charge of refugee policy. Most notable in this latter category according to Morse and others was Breckinridge Long in the State Department, whom Roosevelt had placed in charge of refugee policy. But Long was far from alone. Jews "are at the heart of the problems that disturb the world today," Henry Ford had asserted, in words that Adolf Hitler could have uttered, in his notorious 1921-22 *The International Jew: the World's Foremost Problem:*

> *The immigration problem is Jewish. The money question is Jewish. The tie-up of world politics is Jewish. The terms of the Peace Treaty are Jewish. The diplomacy of the world is Jewish. The moral question in movies and theaters is Jewish. The mystery of the illicit liquor business is Jewish.*[8]

Public opinion polls taken during the 1930s and 1940s consistently indicated more than half of the American population holding negative images of Jews, images that focused on their supposed greed, dishonesty and power in business, finance, government and politics. Indeed, with the exception of 1942, Jews were consistently seen as more of a threat than even the Germans or the Japanese, with more than a third of the population willing to support or sympathize with an anti-Jewish campaign.[9]

Even the small immigration quotas that did exist were not filled. Long and his associates in the State Department demanded completion of fifty pages of documents for anyone wishing to immigrate, including a form four feet long completed on both sides and submitted in six copies (this before copiers existed) with supporting forms that Jews could obtain only from the Nazis. They also had to be able to prove their financial independence, even though the Nazis demanded that departing Jews leave all their property in Germany. The only alternative to such financial independence was American sponsors, who had to prove that they had sufficient financial resources in the midst of the Great Depression as well as a willingness to support the refugee.

Other explanatory factors cited by the critics included bureaucratic blindness in the War Department as well as the State Department and Roosevelt's refusal to deal with the issue—a refusal based partially on faith in his old friend Long and partially due to the fact that FDR usually responded only to political pressure.

Apathetic at best and openly hostile to Jews at worst, the general public clearly would not exert such pressure. Nor would American Jews, primarily as a result of their internal divisions over Zionism vs. assimilation and their desire for acceptance into American life. Many also wished to downplay the "Jewish angle" to the refugee problem due to anti-Semitic attacks being launched against Roosevelt by his enemies, with the New Deal often referred to by those enemies as the "Jew Deal."

Why did such historical attacks on the Roosevelt and American response to the Holocaust appear so suddenly and overwhelmingly between 1968 and 1986? Declassification of key government documents from the World War II era clearly played a role. During those years the State Department published thousands of such documents within its *Foreign Relations of the United States* series and declassified millions more for researchers to use. Equally important, however, was a dramatic decrease in anti-immigrant and anti-Semitic sentiments within the United States. Opposition to Jewish immigration had remained at consistently high levels before, during and immediately after the Second World War, with 60-72 percent opposing Jewish immigration in 1938-39 and again in 1946-47 (interestingly the same time the public voiced overwhelming support for the establishment of Israel—an odd combination of beliefs that most likely expressed sympathy for the survivors of the Holocaust along with no desire to see them come here). Such opposition decreased dramatically, however, during the 1970s and 1980s. Indeed, 1967 witnessed the first major revision of the immigration laws and quotas since the 1920s. By 1984, 79% of those polled favored allowing dissident and persecuted Soviet Jews to enter the country—a complete reversal of the statistics for 1946-47.[10]

Another critical factor was a series of dramatic changes in both the general American and the Jewish American collective memories and cultures during the 1970s and 1980s. As Peter Novick has noted and emphasized, such changes go a long way to explaining why the Holocaust as a whole became a dominant theme and issue within the United States during these years. The two decades witnessed a dramatic decline in what Novick labeled the "integrationist ethos" and its replacement with a "particularist ethos" that focused on what made different Americans unique rather than what united them. The shift in the African American community from civil rights to "Black Power" was both a cause and an effect of this change—a change that in turn fractured the Black-Jewish alliance of the civil rights era. It also fractured the Jewish alliance with Liberal politics, with Black and Leftist attacks in the late 1960s leading many Jews in a rightward direction politically. The 1968 New York City Teachers' Strike was a symbol of this rift and shift.[11]

The shift also coincided with and was reinforced by the Arab-Israeli Six-Day War of 1967, a war whose result turned Israel from fragile and threatened victim into military power and victor as well as occupier. It thereby dramatically decreased Black and Liberal sympathy for the Jewish state and led to attacks on Israel as colonial and racist. For American Jews, however, fear for Israel's survival before and during the war raised the whole issue of Jewish vulnerability once again, followed after the war by a need to justify Israel as a major military power.[12]

For many American Jews, the Holocaust by this time had also replaced religion and culture as the unifying force in their Jewish lives and the core of their particularism. Reinforcing this shift was the fact that victimhood came to be seen as a badge of honor, not shame, within American society as a whole. As Novick has noted, victimhood dramatically changed in American culture during these decades

> *from a status all but universally shunned and despised to one often eagerly embraced. On the individual level, the cultural icon of the strong, silent hero is replaced by the vulnerable and verbose antihero. Stoicism is replaced as a prime value by sensitivity. Instead of enduring in silence, one lets it all hang out. The voice of pain and outrage is alleged to be 'empowering' as well as therapeutic.*

Indeed, assertion of historical victimization, according to Novick, "is always central" to any group's "assertion of its distinct identity."[13]

Major modifications and questioning of the critical interpretation of the U.S. response to the Holocaust began to emerge in the late 1980s with the publication of more balanced and nuanced works by such scholars as Deborah Lipstadt, Richard Breitman and Alan Kraut. It then became a major surge in the 1990s as numerous historians questioned whether the death camps could have been effectively bombed, what was politically as well as militarily possible for the Roosevelt administration between 1933 and 1945, whether substantially more Jews could have been saved, and how bad Roosevelt's record really was—especially in comparison with other major political leaders at that time. By the end of the decade Novick's highly critical work had been published, while another historian had bluntly titled his work *The Myth of Rescue*.[14]

While not going that far, numerous scholars argued that the condemnations of the previous decades were ahistorical in that they had ripped the issue out of its historical context, incorrectly applied the values of the present to a past with different values and priorities ("presentism"), and assumed a power to change events that did not exist. They also faulted those previous condemnations for their incorrect emphasis on certain causative factors. Breitman and Kraut, for example, maintained than anti-Semitism was not central to the shaping of U.S. policy on the issue; instead they focused on a complex interaction between pre-existing immigration restriction laws from the 1920s, public opposition to any increases, an entrenched State Department bureaucracy committed to a narrow defense of U.S. interests, and Roosevelt's reluctance to accept the political risks inherent in supporting measures to help Jews. Others emphasized the fact that no "Holocaust" was taking place in the 1930s—just a Nazi persecution of German Jews, seen as no different from numerous other persecutions, and a resulting refugee problem. The ability to see this persecution as a precursor to the death camps is a luxury of contemporary historical hindsight that was not available or possible in the 1930s.

As for the Holocaust itself, the bulk of Jewish deaths occurred during the years 1941-1943, the worst time in the war for the Allies and the time period in which they had no military power to stop it. Furthermore, Auschwitz was not even known as an extermination center—just one of many concentration camps for Poles—until June of 1944. Even after that discovery it could not have been as easily bombed as the critics maintained due to a host

of operational problems—problems Americans do not recognize
because of a long-standing love affair with, incorrect view of, and
gross overestimation of airpower and what it can accomplish. In
reality, "surgical strike" was and continues to be for all intents and
purposes an oxymoron. Furthermore, Allied air forces were in
1944 stretched to their limits and trying desperately to end the war
in that year—which had they succeeded would have saved more
Jews than any other measures. It is also very questionable how
much the bombing of the Auschwitz gas chambers and rail lines
would have accomplished. The Germans had previously been
able to repair bombed rail lines within 24 hours, and gas chambers were far from the only method the Nazis used to kill Jews.
Indeed, the bombing itself would have killed Jews, both the
World Jewish Congress and the Jewish Agency in Palestine opposed it, and Roosevelt was never even asked to order it.[15]
    Two additional examples of the early critics' misreading of
the present into the past were their assumption of any Jewish
power at this time and the priority that was or should have been
given by the administration to the issue of saving Jews. In truth
Jews were divided, discriminated against, and utterly powerless at
this time, and saving Jews was not at any time the major issue for
Roosevelt or his advisers: dealing with the Great Depression, getting the public to accept U.S. entry into World War II, and winning World War II were. Indeed, Robert Herzstein argued in 1989
that not pushing for revision of the immigration quotas from
1933-1941 was part of the price Roosevelt believed he had to pay
in order to convince an isolationist, anti-immigrant and anti-Semitic American public to enter World War II and defeat Nazi Germany.[16] More recently Richard Breitman similarly noted that,

> *Obstructed for years by a strong isolationist faction in
> Congress, pilloried by right-wing extremists as "Presi-
> dent Rosenfeld," depicted as being surrounded by Jews,
> well aware of a significant anti-Semitic current among
> the American people, and seeing the war as the greatest
> crisis in Western history, FDR reacted as most realistic
> politicians would. He limited is visibility on Jewish issues
> partly in self-defense, partly in the hope that the public
> and Congress would be less likely to object to his defense*

and foreign policies.[17]

And after U.S. entry, other scholars maintain, the best way to save Jews was indeed to win the war as quickly as possible. Furthermore, no policies on saving Jews even existed; instead specific policies developed in response to specific events. Indeed, there is no evidence that alternative policies were possible or would have worked. Former Roosevelt Institute President William J. Vanden Heuvel went even further. In a vigorous defense of FDR published in *American Heritage* in 1999, he argued that Roosevelt did more than any other world leader to save Jews and that during his administration more Jews were let into the United States (approximately 200,000) than into all other countries combined. Furthermore, under Roosevelt's leadership the United States both entered World War II and played a major role in winning it. "We were not their [Nazi's] accomplices," Vanden Heuvel concluded in this regard and in direct response to the early critics; "We destroyed them."[18]

Other scholars emphasized the fact that governments do not sacrifice or even risk the lives of their own citizens to try to save the lives of non-citizens. Nor do they usually undertake humanitarian initiatives outside their own countries. These scholars also noted that wartime reports of the Holocaust were neither believed nor understood. During the interwar years, Americans had learned that World War I reports of German atrocities in Belgium that they had believed at that time had actually been manufactured by the British Government, and they therefore tended to discount these new reports as simply more anti-German propaganda. Furthermore, as Lipstadt, Breitman and Walter Laqueur have all emphasized, there is a huge difference between knowledge and belief, and belief that a supposedly civilized people could actually conduct such mass murder was simply beyond the capacity of most people during World War II. When Supreme Court Justice Felix Frankfurter was informed of the death camps by an eyewitness, he responded that he did not believe the witness but was by no means calling him a liar. "I did not say that he is lying," Frankfurter told the Polish ambassador; "I said I cannot believe him. There is a difference. My mind, my heart, they are made in such a way that I cannot conceive it."[19]

Numerous factors account for this vigorous counterattack against the early critics and defense of FDR in the 1990s. It is generally quite normal in historiography for such a counterattack to take place after the passage of a decade or two. In this particular case, the normal historiographical pattern was probably reinforced by anger over the moralizing in both the PBS television and earlier works, with their focus on *intentions* instead of *results*. (Charles DeGaulle supposedly once commented that only God can judge the former; human beings deal with the latter). What difference, the scholars of the 1990s asked in this regard, would other policies have really made?

There was also anger amongst some historians over the apparent insistence by the early critics that FDR and his associates should have thought in 1930s the way we think today—a form of presentism noted by Lipstadt and others and defined by Michael Marrus as the "historian's form of hubris"—to "denounce the characters we write about for not being like ourselves." Many of these scholars also maintained that the historian's task should be "explanation rather than condemnation." Arthur Schlesinger Jr. aptly combined both criticisms by pungently noting that "Righteousness is easy in retrospect."[20]

Reinforcing these defenses of FDR were the examples during the 1990s of inaction in the face of genocide within Bosnia and Rwanda. Those inactions also revealed the continued difficulty of doing anything effective to stop a genocide, and the ease with which such issues are ignored by people and their governments.

Equally if not more important was a greater focus within the historical profession in general on culture during late 20th century. That focus gave scholars a tool to attack the critics and their interpretations as distortions of the record caused by cultural changes previously discussed[21] and at least partially motivated by contemporary political agendas. Novick in particular made use of Maurice Halbwachs' concept of "collective memory" and the idea that present concerns determine both what of the past we remember and how we remember it. He and others noted in this regard the ahistorical if not anti-historical nature of such memory,[22] and the self-serving misuse of historical analogies to the Holocaust. Orthodox and politically right-wing Jews, Lipstadt concluded, used the critiques of the years 1967-1986 to attack the assimilationist and liberal American Jewish leadership of the Roosevelt era.[23] Novick concluded that the entire focus on the Holocaust was a distorted product of changes in American culture and the fact that the event allowed the entire American political spectrum to draw such self-serving historical analogies. Conservatives have used it to justify anti-Communist interventions, their negative view of human nature, and their opposition to abortion (which they refer to as the "abortion holocaust"). Leftists have used it to bash Liberal icons like FDR who supposedly did nothing to stop it. Liberals have used it to illustrate the evils of immigration restriction, homophobia, nuclear weapons and the Vietnam War. And virtually all Americans have used it as a "moral reference point" to unite them when nothing else could and "for the purpose of self-congratulation: the 'Americanization' of the Holocaust has involved using it to demonstrate the difference between the Old World and the New, and to celebrate, by showing its negation, the American way of life."[24]

The Holocaust is far from the only World War II event to be so misused and manipulated. Indeed, many historians, especially those of us who study US foreign policy and/or World War II, have for decades been rather appalled by the self-serving and distorted analogies to the 1930s and 1940s and ensuing "lessons" that policymakers have used to rationalize and justify their behavior—often with disastrous results.[25] A few years ago I even added a new essay study question that focused on this to the list of such questions I provide students in my foreign relations course before the final exam: discuss the uses and misuses every president from Harry Truman to George W. Bush has made of analogies to the 1930s to justify particular policies.

The process of interpreting and reinterpreting the U.S. response to the Holocaust is far from over. Indeed, our reinterpretations of this issue, as well as others, will always reflect our contemporary concerns and contemporary values. That is part of the historical process. History is not a science. It is a subjective discipline in which we consistently search for roots to contemporary issues and problems and are influenced in our interpretations by those contemporary issues and problems. The U.S. response to the Holocaust was a non-issue for more than twenty years due to specific historical circumstances and became a major issue due to changing circumstances in 1960s and 1970s. It is far from the only such historical subject to move from non-issue to major and controversial issue. Women's history, for example, did not even exist as a field of historical study when I was a student, even though the raw material for its study had always existed. It emerged as a field only during the 1970s, primarily as a result of the women's movement of that decade. As is usual in historiography, some of the work in each school of thought on the U.S. response to the Holocaust has gone overboard. As previously noted, many of the early critics have already been criticized themselves for overstating their attacks on the Roosevelt Administration, and in all likelihood the next generation of historians will in turn reject the more extreme and sweeping of these criticisms during the 1990s and come up with a synthesis. Indeed, that process may have already begun.[26]

What that synthesis will look like is anyone's guess, for it will depend to an extent on future events that no one can see. But let me briefly summarize my present perspective in light of all this past work.

The issue from 1933-41 was one of persecution and immigration, not genocide. US inaction was due to a complex combination of factors.

The base was pre-existing anti-Semitism and nativism. Nativism had previously existed in U.S. history, but its re-emergence at this time resulted from the huge wave of the so-called "new" immigrants from Eastern and Southern Europe in late 19th and early 20th centuries and their association in the American mind with the simultaneous and new problems of industrialization and urbanization that were afflicting American life. Many Americans concluded that these new immigrants were a, if not the major cause of these problems—a belief reinforced by the rise in the 19th century of a new "scientific" racism that argued these new immigrants were inferior and could not be assimilated. Such beliefs resulted in major immigration restriction laws in the 1920s, laws not repealed until 1967. These laws were supported by liberal progressive reformers who wanted to clean up the cities, labor that feared for its jobs, and rural Protestants who feared urban culture.

To that base one must add the Great Depression which high-lighted the job issue, and the rise of a new Nazi-type of anti-Semi-tism on top of older, pre-existing anti-Semitism. This anti-Semi-tism was most clearly expressed by Henry Ford and Father Charles Coughlin, the famous "radio priest" of the era. One must also add American disillusionment in the 1930s with World War I and the consequent resurgence of political isolationism and a de-sire to stay out of any second world war, illustrated in the Neutral-ity Acts of the 1930s, as the war clouds gathered.

Franklin D. Roosevelt was unwilling to challenge any of this—at first because of the primacy of New Deal legislation to combat the Great Depression and his subsequent desire not to alienate any supporters, and by 1940 because of his overriding concern with building a broad coalition in favor of aiding Britain against Germany. His caution was only increased by the fact that some opponents of these policies attacked them as Jewish-in-spired and/or controlled—a fact that also increased the caution of American Jews who at this point faced extensive discrimination and held little if any political power. Furthermore, Roosevelt truly feared possible Nazi subversion via German immigrants. He also feared the power of public opinion to subvert his policies—as it had Woodrow Wilson's policies in 1919-1920. "It is a terri-ble thing," he once stated in this regard, "to look over your shoul-der when you are trying to lead—and to find no one there."[27] Consequently he left the matter largely in the hands of the State Department, whose personnel shared the nativist and anti-Semit-ic sentiments of most Americans and who truly feared Nazi spies and subversives. As a result they used existing immigration laws and bureaucratic procedures to keep Jewish immigration to a min-imum, both before and after U.S. entry into the war.

The shift in Nazi policy from expulsion of Jews to outright murder and genocide coincided with the worst period the war for the Allies, a period in which they were capable of little save avoiding their own defeat. Consequently any rescue of Jews re-mained a very low, indeed a non-existent priority. And while the danger of military defeat had clearly passed by 1944, these prior-ities did not. For Roosevelt, the top priorities were to totally de-feat the Axis powers and to maintain both public and Allied unity in furtherance of that goal. The War Department was set on using all its military resources to achieve that victory as quickly as possible, a goal FDR also supported. Furthermore, it deeply resented any civilian "intrusions" that might distract from that central mission. It also faced very serious military obstacles to bombing the death camps and the probability of high casualties in any effort to do so. That the victims in the camps were not U.S. citizens added another layer of resistance, for nations do not usually sacrifice the lives of their own citizens to save the lives of non-citizens.

Roosevelt thus faced serious bureaucratic resistance from two of his most important wartime departments—State and War—to any effort to rescue Jews. The power of bureaucracies to thwart the policies of their superiors is well-known, and Roosevelt's bureaucracy was particularly chaotic and uncontrollable in this regard. But Churchill faced similar bureaucratic resistance in his desire to bomb Auschwitz. As Richard Breitman has aptly noted, "When dealing with large bureaucracies, even chief executives are not all powerful."[28]

All of these factors must be considered in order to understand American and Allied inaction. No one of them alone can explain it. The "bottom line," however, is that saving European Jewish lives was not a policy priority, or indeed a policy at all, for all of the reasons just cited.

But *could* anything have been done to save more Jews had Roosevelt and the American people possessed the desire and willingness to do so? We will never know, for that is counterfactual, or "what if" history for which there is no historical evidence. Wyman listed twelve programs that could have been tried and that might have worked, but his critics have attacked each of them. What is absolutely clear in hindsight is that no U.S. or Allied action, save stopping Hitler in 1938, could have saved the bulk of European Jewry. Most of those who died in the Holocaust were Jews who fell into his hands after that date and who perished at a time when the United States and its allies were militarily helpless to do anything about it.

Yet it is also clear that *some* could have been saved. In this regard, I am reminded of Yehuda Bauer's response, during the 1991 Hilberg symposium at UVM, to the person in the audience who asserted that U.S. and Allied action could have saved millions of lives. Bauer flatly and heatedly denied that, but then concluded that he came from a Jewish tradition in which to save a single life is to save a whole world. So do I.

Notes:
[1] See my "The United States and Wartime Diplomacy, 1941-1945," in *American Foreign Relations Since 1600: A Guide to the Literature*, 2nd. ed. Robert Beisner (Santa Barbara, CA: ABC Clio, 2003), 1: 1029-33.

[2] Barton Bernstein, "Roosevelt, Truman, and the Atomic Bomb, 1941-1945: A Reinterpretation," *Political Science Quarterly* 90 (Spring, 1975): 23-69; Martin J. Sherwin, *A World Destroyed: The Atomic Bomb and the Grand Alliance* (New York: Knopf, 1975). For the full historiography, see J. Samuel Walker, "The Decision to Use the Atomic Bomb: A Historiographical Update," in *America in the World: The Historiography of American Foreign Relations since 1941*, ed. Michael J. Hogan (New York: Cambridge University Press, 1995), 206-33.

[3] Michael J. Neufeld and Michael Berenbaum, eds., *The Bombing of Auschwitz: Should the Allies Have Attempted It?* (New York: St. Martin's Press, 2000), 3.

[4] "It's your funeral," the adviser Franz Neumann warned. See Raul Hilberg, *The Politics of Memory: The Journey of a Holocaust Historian* (Chicago: Ivan R. Dee, 1996), 66.

[5] Arthur D. Morse, *While Six Million Died: A Chronicle of American Apathy* (New York: Random House, 1967-68); David S. Wyman, *Paper Walls: America and the Refugee Crisis, 1938-1941* (Amherst: University of Massachusetts Press, 1968); Henry Feingold, *The Politics of Rescue: The Roosevelt Administration and the Holocaust, 1938-1945* (New Brunswick, NJ: Rutgers University Press, 1970); Saul S. Friedman, *No Haven for the Oppressed: United States Policy toward Jewish Refugees, 1938-1945* (Detroit: Wayne State University Press, 1973); Herbert Drucks, *The Failure to Rescue* (New York: R. Speller, 1977); Walter Laqueur, *The Terrible Secret: Suppression of the Truth about Hitler's "Final Solution"* (Boston: Little, Brown, 1980); Monty Noam Penkower, *The Jews Were Expendable: Free World Diplomacy and the Holocaust* (Urbana: University of Illinois Press, 1983); Haskel Lookstein, *Were We Our brothers' Keepers? The Public Response*

to the Holocaust, 1938-1944 (New York: Hartmore House, 1985); Rafael Medoff, *The Deafening Silence* (New York: Shapolsky,1987); William Perl, *The Holocaust Conspiracy: An International Policy of Genocide* (New York: Shapolsky,1989). This list is far from complete. For additional titles see the works in my previously-cited "The United States and Wartime Diplomacy," 1029-33.

[6] David S. Wyman, *The Abandonment of the Jews: America and the Holocaust, 1941-1945* (New York: Pantheon Books, 1984).

[7] Robert Dallek, *Franklin D. Roosevelt and American Foreign Policy, 1932-1945* (New York: Oxford University Press, 1979), 166-68, 444-48, 529.

[8] Henry Ford, *The International Jew: the World's Foremost Problem* (Dearborn, MI: Dearborn Publishing Co., 1921-22), 3: 243-44.

[9] See Hadley Cantril, ed., *Public Opinion, 1935-1946* (Princeton, NJ: Princeton University Press, 1951), 382-85, 1150. For summaries of these and other polls, see Richard Breitman, "The Failure to Provide a Safe Haven for European Jewry," in *FDR and the Holocaust*, ed. Verne W. Newton (New York: St. Martin's Press, 1996), 131; and Robert E. Herzstein, *Roosevelt & Hitler: Prelude to War* (New York: Paragon House, 1989), 257.

[10] Ibid., 265.

[11] Peter Novick, *The Holocaust in American Life* (Boston: Houghton Mifflin, 1999), 6-7, 172-73.

[12] Deborah Lipstadt, "The Failure to Rescue and Contemporary American Jewish Historiography of the Holocaust: Judging from a Distance," in Neufeld and Berenbaum, *The Bombing of Auschwitz*, 232-34.

[13] Novick, *The Holocaust in American Life*, 8.

[14] Deborah Lipstadt, *Beyond Belief: The American Press and the Coming of the Holocaust, 1933-1945* (New York: Free Press, 1986); Richard D. Breitman and Alan M. Kraut, *American Refugee Policy and European Jewry, 1933-1945* (Bloomington: Indiana University Press, 1987); William D. Rubinstein, *The Myth of Rescue: Why the Democracies Could Not Have Saved More Jews from the Nazis* (New York: Routledge, 1997). For comprehensive summaries of this new scholarship, see Newton, FDR

and the Holocaust, and Neufeld and Berenbaum, *The Bombing of Auschwitz.*

[15] Ibid.

[16] Herzstein, *Roosevelt & Hitler.*

[17] Richard Breitman, "Roosevelt and the Holocaust," in Newton, *FDR and the Holocaust* 114.

[18] William J. Vanden Heuvel, "America and the Holocaust," *American Heritage* 50 (July/August 1999): 38-52

[19] Peter Grose, *Israel in the Mind of America* (New York: Alfred A. Knopf, 1983), 132-33. See also Laqueur, *The Terrible Secret* pp. 3, 237.

[20] Lipstadt, "The Failure to Rescue," 235; Michael R. Marrus, "Bystanders to the Holocaust," and Arthur Schlesinger, Jr., "Did FDR Betray the Jews," in Newton, *FDR and the Holocaust*, 152, 160-61

[21] See above, pp. 4-6.

[22] Novick, *The Holocaust in American Life*, 3-6.

[23] Lipstadt, "The Failure to Rescue," 231-34.

[24] Novick, *The Holocaust in American Life*, 12-13.

[25] See, for ex., Ernest R. May, *"Lessons" of the Past: the Use and Misuse of History in American Foreign Policy* (New York: Oxford University Press, 1973) and, more recently, Jeffrey Record, *The Specter of Munich: Reconsidering the Lessons of Appeasing Hitler* (Washington, DC: Patomac Books, 2007).

[26] See in this regard Walter Laqueur's critical review of Rubinstein's *Myth of Rescue*, "No Exit?" in *Commentary* (October 1997): 59-62.

[27] Justus D. Doenecke and John E. Wilz, *From Isolation to War, 1931-1941* 3rd. ed. (Arlington Heights, IL: Harlan Davidson, 2003), 75-76.

[28] Breitman, "Roosevelt and the Holocaust," 122. Breitman cites in this regard Martin Gilbert, *Auschwitz and the Allies* (New York: Holt, Rinehart and Winston, 1981), esp. 267-76.

"To Leave or Not to Leave – That was Just One of the Questions": Jewish Emigration from the Third Reich

David Scrase

Introduction

The nineteenth annual Harry H. Kahn Memorial Lecture was presented on April 7, 2008, and we were delighted to have our very own Prof. David Scrase from the Department of German and Russian at the University of Vermont be the distinguished speaker. For close to four decades he has been a stalwart of German and Holocaust studies on this campus.

Let me start my short introductory comments by stating that they represent the collective view of the faculty and students of the Department of German and Russian and the Center for Holocaust Studies. We all respect, admire, and treasure Prof. David Scrase for his over thirty-five years of dedicated teaching, engaged scholarship, and valuable service at the University of Vermont. He has educated and mentored many eager students of German and Holocaust studies on both the undergraduate and graduate levels, and he has had a special influence on them intellectually and ethically.

A mere glance at his impressive curriculum vitae with its eighteen authored, edited and translated books reveals that Prof. Scrase is a nationally and internationally recognized scholar in the fields of poetry, modern German literature, the art of translation, the literature of former East Germany, and the Holocaust. He has published widely in these five scholarly areas, many times linking all of them into a cohesive whole. He began his life-long interest in the northern German poet Wilhelm Lehmann with his dissertation on *The Dialectic in Wilhelm Lehmann's Nature Imagery* that was completed in 1972 at Indiana University. In 1984 he wrote the definitive book on *Wilhelm Lehmann: A Critical Biography* that was followed by the edition of a massive volume of Wilhelm Lehmann's *Gesammelte Werke*. *Erzählungen* (1994) and his valuable book on *Understanding Johannes Bobrowski* (1995). His numerous articles on modern German authors include such names as Johannes Bobrowski, Ludwig Greve, Joseph Hahn, Stephan Hermlin, Paul Nizon, Peter Schneider, and Anna Seghers. While his literary scholarship is impeccable, he also deserves highest praise as the editor and translator of poetry and fiction, among them entire books of aphorisms and poetry or long novels by Marie von Ebner-Eschenbach, Phia Rilke, Ilse Tielsch, and Joseph Hahn.

The work of this untiring scholar has been supported by Fulbright and Alexander von Humboldt fellowships as well as UVM research grants and richly deserved sabbaticals. Let me also mention his over one hundred reviews of Austrian, German, and Swiss literary works by modern authors. These reviews all appeared in the international journal *World Literature Today*, and taken as a whole, they represent a history of major literary works in the German language of the past four decades—a truly remarkable and unique accomplishment.

Prof. Scrase's activities as the founding Director of the Center for Holocaust Studies are indeed exemplary. During his fourteen years from 1993 to 2006 as director he was also the editor of the influential *Bulletin of the Center for Holocaust Studies at the University of Vermont*, and his three edited books on *The Holocaust: Introductory Essays* (1996), *The Holocaust: Personal Accounts* (2001), and *Making A Difference: Rescue and Assistance During the Holocaust* (2004) have reached many students and teachers in the state of Vermont and throughout the country. He also edited *Reflections on the Holocaust* (2001), a special volume honoring Prof. Raul Hilberg on his seventy-fifth birthday.

As a teacher, mentor, and advisor Prof. Scrase has also distinguished himself due to his keen and inquisitive mind, his encyclopedic knowledge of German art, culture, history, music, and literature, and his ability to engage his students in a meaningful educational discourse. He is known as a professor of highest standards, a teacher who expects much of his students—and yes, someone who does pay attention to such matters as the precision and correctness of language. While dealing with various subject matters, Prof. Scrase's students will always also be challenged to write the best of prose, both stylistically and grammatically. But it is, of course, the intellectual content that he is after, and Prof. Scrase most certainly challenges his students to expand their minds, to think critically, to broaden their analytical skills, and to think in an inclusive fashion. Little wonder that Prof. Scrase was also hailed as a superb director of our study-abroad program at the University of Salzburg at Austria. There too he quickly gained the trust and respect by students from numerous New England universities, and they treasured him both as a sincere advisor and demanding instructor. Students on our campus, i.e., German majors, Holocaust Studies minors, first year students, and also graduate students flock to Prof. Scrase for instruction and advice.

His teaching and scholarship are augmented by a much-appreciated dedication to service of various types, ranging from his former directorship of the German House Program to being the faculty advisor of the UVM Rugby Team. Prof. Scrase's untiring efforts for his students and the Holocaust Center also lead him to organize numerous lectures, symposia, and film screenings. Add to this a multitude of committee memberships, review boards, evaluations of manuscripts, editorial services, and various other meaningful and necessary assignments, including his most successful fund-raising efforts for the Center of Holocaust Studies, and you have a solid picture of Prof. David Scrase who has been in the teaching profession since 1962, when he began to instruct students in Germany after having graduated from Bristol University in his native England. Forty-five years before the mast, so to speak, and still weathering the deep seas of teaching, steering the boat of his students with a firm but kind hand and a bit of a stiff upper lip, as is befitting to this scholar and gentleman from the British Isles.

Suffice it to say that Prof. David Scrase represents the very best among us. We take pride in his accomplishments in the field of German language, culture, and literature, and we applaud his untiring efforts on behalf of the Humanities. Above all we will forever be thankful to him for having created and directed the UVM Center for Holocaust Studies—an invaluable achievement and lasting legacy.

Lecture[1]

Given today's subject, it would be remiss of me, I feel, if I did not say a few words about the emigration of Irene and Harry Kahn, for whom this lecture series is named and whose legacy we are here to honor. Irene, by the way, is ninety-three years old. I spoke with her a few weeks ago and know that she, although unable to be here in person, is certainly with us in spirit today.

For the Jews in Germany emigration was the official policy of the Nazis until October 1941 and was seen as the solution to the "Jewish problem." Indeed about 37,000 Jews left Germany in 1933, the first year of the National Socialist regime. Seemingly, their minds were soon made up, there were no questions. But for the Kahns[2] it was not so easy. Harry had trained to be a teacher at a Jewish teachers' training college in Würzburg. He then taught in Jewish schools, at that time still under the control of the state-run system. It soon came to the point where he had no rights as a civil servant, but was still employed and paid by the system. Both Harry and Irene lived in Baden-Württemberg, and it was here that both were employed—Harry in Baisingen, where he grew up, and then later in nearby Rexingen, where Irene came from. Irene worked in a bank, until she was fired in1934. The bank manager soon wanted her back and offered her her old position, but in an office in the back, where she would not be seen. She declined this offer and went to work for a Jewish firm. As Irene states at the beginning of her piece in our book *Personal Accounts*: "[a]t this time [i.e.1933] I was not even considering emigration. My father was blind, and I felt there was no way I could leave Germany and leave him behind" (Scrase/Mieder, p.1). However, as things got steadily worse, and after the death of her father in 1935, her mother wrote to relatives in the USA in order to obtain the requisite affidavit. The plan was that her mother would stay in Germany until Irene was in the States, at which point she would be better placed to arrange for her mother's passage. The receipt of an affidavit, however, did not preclude a wait of months or even years before one received a visa and could leave. The question of the quota and of a number was a further frustration. But the affidavit did arrive and the next step toward a visa was undertaken. Meanwhile Harry was taking a similar path, although he had no relatives in the U.S. Accordingly his affidavit eventually came from a Jewish family in

Boston, who did not know him. But I am getting ahead of myself. By this time, it was 1938. Jewish passports had been stamped with a large "J," Jews were now obliged to add the name Israel for men and Sarah for women, and, by the end of the year, the *Kristallnacht* pogrom had taken place. The situation was becoming dire. Their chosen strategy in these circumstances was not uncommon. Rather than stay in Germany, they would go abroad with some kind of temporary visa while they waited for their visa to the U.S. As a young woman, Irene would find it relatively easy to go to Britain as a house-keeper/governess and await the visa there. This she did, spending ten months in Shirehampton near Bristol. (About 14,000 German-Jewish women went to Britain as housekeepers or nannies.) Between Irene's departure by train and ferry for England in February 1939 and the outbreak of the war in September, Harry was able to follow her, with the help of a cousin living in England. Harry left Rexingen for Switzerland, which was the closest foreign country, albeit over a hundred and fifty miles to the south. Remarkably a Rexingen taxi driver was willing to drive him to Lörrach on the Swiss border—a dangerous act of kindness in the circumstances.[3]   Harry left Germany in June 1939. They both had visas for Switzerland, France, and Belgium, which suggests that they traveled via those three countries to avoid extensive travel through Germany. The ferry would have then taken them from Ostende to England.

Without a position in England, Harry was obliged to stay in London at Woburn House, which was the seat of both the German-Jewish Aid Committee and the Central Office for Refugees, and which functioned as a refugee relief centre. Woburn House in 1939 was inundated with enquiries (more than 1,000 letters, telegrams, and telephone calls arrived daily). The Kahns' care in leaving Germany while they waited for their papers to come through paid off, for they were outside Germany when war came in September 1939. Even so, Harry was obliged to find someone in England to vouch for him and confirm his status as a political refugee. A rabbi in London obliged. The visas arrived in the fall of 1939 and the couple was able to leave Liverpool on board the ship "Georgic," which set off for New York City in a blacked-out convoy in December, docking in New York in January 1940. They lived and worked in New York City, where their daughter Hazel was born, until 1944, when they moved to Vermont. Here their son Max was born. Here they became citizens in 1945, and here they joined the Ohavi Zedek community, where Harry headed the Hebrew school until he joined the faculty of UVM in 1948. Incidentally, just after *Kristallnacht* the local *Landjäger*, a kind of gendarme, came to Harry and Irene with the torah salvaged from the ruins of the pogrom. They were able to bring it with them to the US, and it is now to be found in the Ohavi Zedek synagogue here in Burlington.

This brief account makes it sound relatively straightforward, almost routine; it could be seen to be a matter of knowing what to do, and how to react, a matter of patience. But it does not begin to describe what it took to come to the decision to leave. Neither does it describe the agony of waiting, the political and financial uncertainties, the possibility of failure, the worry about loved ones, the concern about the future, and coping with a foreign language and culture, to name just a few of the problems. In terms of financial uncertainty and the worry about one's relatives, disaster soon struck the Kahns. In trying to get papers for Irene's mother, still living in Germany, Harry and Irene heard about a man who could secure visas for Cuba. They dipped into their meager savings and paid for the "service." The papers never arrived, the money and the man were never seen again. Worse yet, when the deportation order reached Irene's mother, she took her own life, and thus evaded murder at the hands of the Nazis after the deportation to Riga.

A willingness to leave, a decision to leave would come to naught if there were no place to go. Choosing your destination required knowledge of which nations were willing to accept refugees, and how many they would accept. The readiness to accept Jews from Germany changed from year to year. The number of nations willing and able to take Jewish refugees dwindled until it was reduced to one city with its peculiar international status—Shanghai. Moreover the quotas varied too from nation to nation. So where you were born became an essential element in the chase for visas. Dr. Otto Ehrenreich, a Viennese physician, was able to leave earlier than he would have left given the combined German-Austrian quota, because, having been born in Trieste, which was part of Italy in the 1930s, he came under the Italian quota.

The brief account of the Kahns' emigration also fails to describe the full extent of the bureaucratic process. Nor does it tell us what *others* did, how many German Jews fled, when they fled, and to where. In fact the statistics are of necessity complex. Even the Nazis remained for a long time unsure about how to deal with the so-called "Mischlinge" or the products of mixed marriages. Are they included in the statistics? And are the non-Jewish spouses in mixed marriages counted? And what about those who left early only to return to Germany later, perhaps to stay there, or perhaps to re-emigrate at a later date? The following are the figures as they appear in the *Columbia Guide to the Holocaust* (Niewyk/Nicosia p. 419):

Year	High Estimate	Low Estimate
1933	63,400	37,000
1934	45,000	22,000
1935	35,000	20,000
1936	34,000	24,000
1937	23,500	23,000
1938	49,000	34,000
1939	68,000	68,000
Totals	318,400	228,000

It is interesting to note how the gap between the high and the low estimates narrows and then suddenly disappears. But what is perhaps most striking is that the 1933 figures are not exceeded until 1939, when the *Kristallnacht* pogrom forced the issue.

Like Harry and Irene, many others did not initially entertain emigration as an option. But if they did wish to emigrate and, unlike Irene Kahn, did not have relatives willing to provide the affidavit, they would be obliged to approach complete strangers and beg for help. In many instances would-be emigrants would leaf through telephone books looking for anyone of the same name who might be willing (and able) to provide an affidavit. Or they would attempt to obtain an affidavit through friends of friends. Harry exemplifies this approach. Both Harry and Irene had the foresight to get out of Germany and wait in safety for the arrival of their visas, which in fact did not arrive until after the beginning of the war. Others, left waiting in Germany, were overtaken by events and suffered the fate of millions. But the visa and the affidavit were only two of the documents required for emigration to the U.S. There was, as the historian David Wyman described it, a veritable "paper wall"[4] that had to be scaled or penetrated before one emigrated. In the application for a visa, of which five copies were demanded (and, remember, these were pre-xerox days) the following items were required:

- Two copies of the birth certificate (important because the quota was based on one's country of birth)
- Proof of the quota number
- Certificate of good conduct from the police, which would include the police dossier, prison record, and military record
- Other government records about the individual
- Affidavits and, after 1940, affidavits of good conduct
- Proof of a successful physical at one of the four U.S. consulates that dealt with all visa applications
- Proof of permission to leave Germany (after 30 September 1939)
- Proof of a booked passage (after September 1939)

Bear in mind that these were the expectations of the U.S. State Department. Jews in Greater Germany were also at the mercy of a regime that, while officially "encouraging" emigration, was at the same time expropriating would-be emigrants to an ever-increasing degree. One must also bear in mind that the number of countries that accepted immigrants was never great and also diminished as time went on. The declaration of war, of course, was another impediment and, as Germany invaded and occupied its neighbors, there were soon almost no havens left. Here are just a few more considerations relating to the question "To leave or not to leave": At the Evian Conference, proposed by FDR and held in the French spa-town of Evian in July 1938 with the purpose of finding solutions to the growing problem of Jews seeking to leave the Greater German Reich, the thirty-two countries participating declared almost unanimously that they had no room for more. Roosevelt's statement that the U.S. would remove the barriers in the way of visa applicants so that the current quotas could be sooner reached did not amount to much, because no increase in those quotas was envisioned. Australia, which, incidentally, apologized in 2008 to its native population for its own history of racial persecution, announced at that time that it had no racial problems and did not wish to import any. Only the Dominican Republic responded positively by stating that they would accept Jewish immigrants and, moreover, provide tracts of agricultural land for them. The Dominican dictator, Trujillo, wanted to improve both agriculture and the economy and his civil rights record, which had suffered because of his persecution of black minorities during the 1930s. There was a price for this generous offer, and the cost involved was borne by the *American Jewish Joint Distribution Committee*, usually known simply as the "Joint."5 About 3,000 Jewish lives were saved through emigration to the Dominican Republic.

You will, of course, by now be thinking "But what about Palestine?" And Palestine was indeed a key player in emigration from Germany—or rather the British were, for they called the shots in regard to Palestine because of their mandate through the League of Nations. In terms of the numbers (and I am again relying on Niewyk and Nicosia), about 53,430 German Jews reached Palestine between 1933-1939—about the same number as reached North America (57,189) and South America (53,472) during the same period. Almost half of the Jews who left Germany before the outbreak of war went to other European countries (153,767). About 40,000 German Jews went to the UK (Niewyk/Nicosia, p. 419). The situation for Jews wishing to emigrate to Palestine was complex, and I won't go into it in any depth, since Frank Nicosia spoke of the "illusion and reality" of the relationship of the Zionists and the Nazis in the Kahn Lecture of 2005. What I do intend to do is to describe some of the reasons, motivations, and experiences of emigrants who, for the most part, chose the Palestine route. They exemplify the differences and the similarities in the emigrants and give a retrospective view of how it was for them.

Just as the U.S. had quotas for immigrants, so, too, did the British in regard to Palestine. Instead of the visa and the affidavit the British issued "Certificates." For ardent Zionists, that is to say for those Jews who did not see an end to anti-Semitism through assimilation or emancipation, but felt that a healthy Jewry would exist only through a clearly defined Jewish identity and through their own nation, Palestine proved not only the only possibility of their own independent nation but also the best way to avoid the reassertion of anti-Semitism in the Nazi state. The promise of such a homeland nation had been put forward in writing by the British in 1917 with the Balfour Declaration, so was the situation in the 1930s not an ideal opportunity to make that nation a reality? Zionists had already been settling in Palestine during the Weimar Republic and this emigration surged somewhat in the Third Reich. The Nazis encouraged emigration to Palestine and through the Haavara Agreement of August 1933 allowed German Jews to take some of their assets to Palestine in the form of German goods, which they bought in Germany and sent to Palestine. There were some mutual "benefits" in this situation: the Germans were able to rid themselves of Jews while retaining their assets in the form of money spent in Germany; Jews were able to leave with goods that were useful to them in their new lives or goods that they could perhaps sell in Palestine, and then use the money to enable them to become more quickly established. But the British were never able to issue enough certificates and had their own quota limits. Furthermore, the British recognized (or were made to recognize) the fears of Arabs, who saw their own position threatened by the new immigrants.

We can clearly see at this point that some of the questions regarding whether to leave were raised, and resolved, because of personal reasons—Irene Kahn could not envisage leaving her blind father alone. Harry, on the other hand, found it perhaps easier to leave for a new chapter of life with Irene, his fiancée. Those with family members abroad, those who had already made the step or had already in the 1920s considered emigration, left almost immediately. Jehuda Ludwig Pfeuffer (born in 1924) describes his family's experience: "My father was a businessman in Würzburg. My grandparents on both sides of the family, my mother's side and my father's, were country Jews, small communities, very orthodox, and they lived like German peasants and looked like German peasants, and were very much orthodox Jews. And we are, I think, one of the few Jewish clans from Germany who all left for Palestine between '33 and '35, ten large families.

Not one stayed behind" (Betten/Du-Nour, p. 39). Pfeuffer is better known today as Jehuda Amichai, the writer.

Younger German Jews, or those who were by nature adventurous, also came more easily to a decision to leave. Others, older, with businesses they had built up, with properties they had worked hard for, were inclined to stay—at least for a bit. After all, Hitler could not last, no other politician had recently led the country for more than a short period. Governments had come and gone with monotonous regularity throughout the 1920s and into the 1930s. Surely, it was reasoned by many, Hitler was no exception. He would soon be found incompetent and there would be a new chancellor and a new government. Alas, they were wrong.

Timing was often also a compelling factor. The Nuremberg Laws of September 1935 gave pause for thought, but the relaxation of anti-Jewish measures because of the 1936 Olympics was seen by some as a sign of hope. The increase in anti-Jewish actions in 1937 and, in particular, 1938 led some to think more seriously that it might be time to leave. The culmination of such anti-Jewish actions in 1938 was, of course, *Kristallnacht* with the massive detentions, arrests, and incarcerations. Conditions for release included a commitment to leave Germany; the decision to leave was, in effect, made for many and the figures for emigration reflect this.

But much earlier, in the first months of the National Socialist Regime, some found the decision to be easy and in a way made for them, too. Famous musicians, like Otto Klemperer or Bruno Walter, had often performed abroad. They had international reputations, contacts, and a clear incentive in that they were forbidden to perform only weeks after Hitler came to power. Similarly, the composer Kurt Weill, fresh from his success with *The Threepenny Opera*, also left in 1933. The famous author, Thomas Mann, who had received the Nobel Prize for Literature only a few years earlier in 1929, was not Jewish but in danger because of his anti-Hitler stance. In January 1933 he was coincidentally abroad—and stayed there. The playwright Bertolt Brecht, who wrote the text to *The Threepenny Opera*, was also not Jewish, but, as a communist, he too was a marked man. He chose to leave immediately. But what about the "ordinary German Jews," if I may put it that way, who opted to leave Germany for Palestine? In what follows, much of my information comes from a book published in Germany in 1995 and curiously unknown in this country. The book, unavailable in English, is called *Wir sind die Letzten. Fragt uns aus*, or We are the Last. You Can Ask Us Anything. Its subtitle runs *Gespräche mit den Emigranten der dreissiger Jahre in Israel*, or Conversations in Israel with the Emigrants of the Thirties. It consists of extracts from interviews made, mostly, in Israel. The individuals who were interviewed vary in age from sixty-five to ninety-seven at the time they were interviewed in the early 1990s. The book is divided into five sections, the second of which is entitled "A New Life." It was this section that proved most useful for the purposes of this talk.

When dealing with memory, there is one thing that must be emphasized: memory is unreliable. Again and again Holocaust witnesses demonstrate this. However, we cannot do without it. Documented fact will not give us the full story, and where we use only documented fact the human element will be lacking—at least to some degree. Statistics and documents tell us how many left, where they went, what they overcame. But witness accounts tell us what the refugees felt, how they changed or were forced to change, how they came to their decisions—and not just in one instance but over a period of years. This is why I remain fixated on the personal accounts. Here are a few interesting examples.

A significant number of the 156 émigrés interviewed for this book and who all ended up in Palestine/Israel did not at first intend to leave Germany. The rationale in the early period of the Third Reich usually ran something like this: "Hitler won't last that long; we have our own lives, businesses, friends, careers" and so on, or "I served with distinction in World War I. they won't touch me." But there is often a qualification that plays a major role. For example, Ada Neumark (Brodsky), born in 1924, who left for Palestine with her parents in 1938, states: "My parents stayed behind much longer than others of our family living in Germany because my father said 'if we leave, that will emphasize, as it were, that we do not believe that things will change.' He was absolutely convinced that the whole thing was just a cloud that would soon pass [....] 'We all have to stand firm until it gets better'" (Betten/Du-nour, p.131). The situation of the Brodsky family was complicated by the fact that Ada's mother came from a

Zionist family and was in favor of leaving immediately. Her father prevailed—for a while. The children, including Ada, went to Palestine early in 1938 with the Youth Aliyah, but their parents came later, after her father was released from a concentration camp.

He is not untypical. The men were often more inclined to stay—or less inclined to go. Gustav Landau was twenty-three when on the day of the boycott of 1 April 1933 his mother announced that they would leave. His father responded, as Landau put it, by more or less saying that she was nuts: "Du bist wohl verrückt geworden." She was not to be deterred, "if we don't leave now", she responded, "it will be too late," and she marched up the stairs to her own mother, who was over seventy. "Now listen to me, Mother, we're going to Palestine. Want to come? And she said 'Ja.'" Gustav or Gad, as he called himself in Israel, tried to put the age factor into context by saying that seventy in those days was "uralt," or "ancient." They then asked whether Gustav wanted to join them, and he, too, thought they were nuts, and stayed. Gustav's mother was a forceful lady and she soon brought her husband round. Indeed, her insistence that this was the right decision was so strong that her husband seems to have resisted considerable pressure on the part of friends, colleagues, and his business partner to stay. Grandmother, mother, father, a sister, and a brother all left within ten days. Gustav finished his studies and joined them before the end of that same year, 1933 (Betten/Du-nour, p. 128). Marion Kaplan has persuasively shown that the women of many families were often the decision-makers.

A good example of a split family with one part wanting to leave and one part wanting to stay for reasons connected with one's business is the Lerner family. A sister living in Berlin left for Palestine in 1936. Her brother, living in Mährisch Ostrau, or Ostrova in Moravia, had a business there. Before the Germans annexed that territory he expanded the business and built a new wing to the factory. When his sister visited him there in 1937, she urged him to forget "mere bricks and mortar and go to Palestine." His response indicates that a business is not just a financial investment: "Now look here, we've built a factory here. I'd love to go, but it's not so easy. There's a deal of work in that factory, a chunk of my life." His son, at the time twenty-seven years old, sums up the situation by emphasizing not the money but the creative work behind it. When they came to the decision to leave it was already too late. They were caught up in the deportations from Ostrava, and spent time in several camps, before escaping and going underground. They survived and finally reached Palestine via Hungary and Italy in 1946 (Betten/Du-nour, p.133).

The camp or prison experience was a great persuader. Mirjam Kedar (b. 1922) was sixteen years old when her father was, "of course," as she put it, incarcerated following the *Kristallnacht* pogrom in 1938. It was only then, she thought, that he really became aware that he could not stay any longer. They had already been obliged to move several times (always a step down, of course, in terms of space, comfort, and convenience). They had already become aware of suicides, which indicated how others felt and yet he still believed that nothing would happen to him. He was, after all, as he continually said: "a German, born in Germany, grown up there, and a World War I veteran who had served at the front." Furthermore, his wife was a Christian. Nothing would happen to them—even though his wife (to please her father-in-law) had converted to Judaism. Slowly, in the course of the year 1938 before *Kristallnacht*, he began to think of leaving. His daughter, the sixteen-year-old Mirjam, left in 1938. Her father did not make it (Betten/Du-nour, p.133-34).

The prison experience was also the compelling factor for the Jensen family. Jutta Jensen (now Jutta Grünthal) describes how her parents and younger siblings left already in 1933 after her "father had been in prison several months." She followed in 1935. It is often assumed that the early emigrants to Palestine must have been Zionists, but her parents were not. The imprisonment made it clear to her father that "one should not merely leave Germany for somewhere else in Europe, but one should leave Europe as well" (Betten/Du-nour, p.134). In 1939 Alice Schwarz-Gardos also decided to leave for Palestine. This was after she had lived and studied first in Vienna, and then in Czechoslovakia. She had seen both domiciles swallowed up into the Greater German Reich: "I wanted to go to Palestine, quite simply because I was convinced after mature reflection that there was no sense in going from one exile into the next" (Betten/Du-nour, p. 134).

Highly educated Europeans who wished to come to the U.S.

in the sixties were part of what was usually called the "brain drain." With Palestine in the 1930s, the situation was the opposite. It was known as the "Jewish pyramid." "This," as Michael Walter explains, "is an upside-down pyramid; where the point is, at the bottom, there are just a few peasants and workers. Up at the top there is a huge number of highly educated intellectuals etc. And that's what the Zionists wanted to turn around!" (Betten/Du-nour, p. 99). Palestine and the British mandate authorities did not want the highly educated. They wanted farm laborers, artisans, skilled workers to be sure, but not, above all, physicians. In Germany and throughout Europe, there existed therefore the possibility of "Um-schulung," or "Umschichtung." The highly educated went to work in camp situations where they learned how to farm, or acquired a new trade that would make them more attractive in the search for a certificate. Erwin Jacobi, with a doctorate in musicology, went to Palestine after such a course and became a chicken farmer. After the war he eventually returned, not to Frankfurt, where he hailed from, but to Switzerland, where he became a world-renowned musicologist.[6] Some were able to revert to their former occupations, others remained in their newly chosen careers.

As time went on, the decision to emigrate may have become easier, but the possibility of getting out decreased and finally, in October 1941, disappeared almost entirely, when Himmler decreed that emigration was prohibited. As Abraham Friedländer (b. 1916), who left in 1936, states: "You went to all the consulates in Germany looking for a visa, whether it was for South America or Shanghai.[7] But it was extremely difficult to get out of Germany to safety. If you wanted to go to Palestine, you were at the mercy of the English mandate authorities who distributed their certificates according to their quota to members of specific groups [...] or you got one of those 'capitalist certificates,' which meant that you had to be able to slap down a good 1,000 pounds sterling. The limit on immigration for Palestine was of course one reason why many were unable to escape the Holocaust" (Betten/Du-nour, p. 135).

The situation with the "capitalist certificates" was interesting: essentially it meant that those who were rich had an easier time getting out than those who were poor. But Erwin (later Elchanan)

Scheftelowitz, born in 1911 in Berlin, has a fascinating story to tell regarding such certificates for those who did not possess the thousand pounds sterling. He had a relative in Switzerland who opened an account in his name which purportedly contained more than one thousand pounds. It was unclear to Scheftelowitz where this considerable amount of money came from. But he was able to take an official Swiss bank statement attesting to his account's value. This is how Scheftelowitz told his story: "I still have this bank note, which is unique, a false statement from a Swiss bank [he laughs]. There at the top of the form is my name, 'Herr Dr. Erwin Scheftelowitz. We certify that you have a deposit at this bank of over one thousand pounds sterling" There is, to be sure, a second sentence, which ran: 'This statement is valid for one month from the date of issue '—I finally learned the answer to this riddle fifteen years ago. I was traveling in Switzerland when someone said 'You know we did quite a lot for refugees. We got them certificates.' I pricked up my ears. In '37, apparently, there was this Jew in South America who had pots of money. He had a huge bank account here in Switzerland, which he never touched. He had a cousin who hit upon the idea of using this dormant account for provisional accounts that were valid for one month. There was a gentleman's agreement, that no one would withdraw any of this money, and that was the solution to this riddle" (Betten/Du-nour, p. 138).

Necessity is the mother of invention. Some took the path, where it existed, of marriage. If a single person had the necessary papers, those who had none could resort to a "Scheinehe," a sham marriage. It is, I believe, generally known that the poet W.H. Auden, who was gay, married Erika Mann, the daughter of Thomas Mann, to give her an easy way into the U.S. in 1935. Some, who were already dating, could proceed to marriage with a degree of confidence. But what of those who did not even know the other person? Gertrud Channa Großmann (b. 1921) left Teplitz-Schönau in Bohemia, which was taken over by the Germans in 1938, for Prague, which was soon incorporated into the Reich the following year. A member of a youth group in Prague, she and some other girls were unable to be spirited out of the city to safety elsewhere—something the youth group was attempting to achieve. So instead the youth group sought out unmarried men, who already had certificates for Palestine through their families. "And there I was, along with five other girls, I believe, in a sham marriage with some young bachelor. I was eighteen and he was, I believe, thirty-five or perhaps a bit younger. But as far as I was concerned he was an old man and my parents thought so, too. My parents were none too pleased, but it was a good thing I did so. The English government knew what was going on, and after two years I was divorced" (Betten/Du-nour, p. 141). Lisalotte Salomon, born in Berlin in 1907, received her certificate just after she began to date a young man. "He said: Can I travel on your certificate?" That was a marriage proposal. And he would have perished if I hadn't said yes. In 1938 his parents came to visit us in Palestine and tried to get us to come back to Germany. His father was a physician, my new husband, too, and they could have worked in the same practice. We stayed here [in Palestine] and they went back. No one knows what happened to them" (Betten/Du-nour, p. 140-41). Well, we know what happened to them, we just do not know where, when, or the precise details.

This next case, my last example, almost seems unbelievable, but here it is. A young man, Moshe Moritz Cederbaum, twenty-three years old emigrated to Palestine via France in 1933-34. Here he went through a sham marriage with a woman who was an illegal immigrant, the idea being that she could then live openly in Palestine and travel legally to and from Europe, indeed to and from Germany. The purpose of these journeys was to take back to Palestine numerous children. In exchange for the favor Cederbaum extended to her through this marriage, she would bring the four children of his uncle, four cousins in other words, back from Germany to the safety of Palestine. But his aunt and uncle, the parents of these four children, ultimately would not allow the children to leave. They feared that the children would not receive a sufficiently "Jewish" education there. By the time they changed their minds in 1942, it was, of course, too late and all were deported to their deaths.

To conclude: There were so many factors at play in the decision whether to leave or not to leave. These factors involved timing, age, finances, religious beliefs, connections, the family situation, flexibility, and historical developments. A sense of, or a readiness for, adventure, and adaptability were often crucial. In the final analysis, however, the decision to leave was not in itself sufficient, if you did not have a place to go. Those places steadily dwindled as the readiness to leave increased. The result was, as we know, catastrophic and tragic.

Notes:
[1] I unwittingly "stole" the first part of my title from my friend and colleague Konrad Kwiet, whose article "To Leave or Not to Leave. The German Jew at the Crossroads" appeared in Walter H. Pehle (ed.), *November 1938—From Reichskristallnacht to Genocide*. New York/Oxford: Berg, 1991.

[2] I am most grateful to the two children of Harry and Irene Kahn for the information and pictures they were able to provide me with.

[3] Rexingen, whither Harry moved to be closer to Irene, was a remarkable small German town. A third of its inhabitants was Jewish. Jews and gentiles got along, and had done so for centuries. A descendant of a Rexingen Jew who left the town and settled in the US, Mimi Schwartz, was so intrigued by her father's stories about life there in the 1930s that she conducted research on the subject for twelve years, writing a book entitled *Good Neighbors, Bad Times.* Perhaps the driver could be fairly certain that friends and neighbors would not denounce him, but there were others that might have found out, people from the area like those who came in from Stuttgart on *Kristallnacht* and torched the synagogue. To drive a Jew from Rexingen to the Swiss border was a dangerous act in the Germany of the late 1930s, no matter where you lived. In her book Schwartz uses fictitious names for the town and its inhabitants.

[4] Chapter 7 of Wyman's book *The Abandonment of the Jews: America and the Holocaust, 1941-1945* bears the title "Paper Walls and Paper Plans."

[5] For more information on this rescue effort, see Marion A. Kaplan. *Dominican Haven: The Jewish Refugee Settlement in Sosúa, 1940-1945.*

[6] Conversation with Dr. Erwin R. Jacobi, a personal friend.

[7] Before World War I there were about 700 Jews living in Shanghai. That number increased considerably after an influx of Jews fleeing the Russian Revolution and then the Third Reich.

Emigration from Germany continued until Himmler's 1941 decree. Shanghai was a free port, which meant that one needed no visa for entry—hence the popularity of Shanghai as a goal for those fleeing Hitler at the last moment.

Works Cited:
Betten, Anne and Mirjam Du-nour (eds.). *Wir sind die Letzten. Fragt uns aus: Gespräche mit den Emigranten der dreissiger Jahre in Israel.* Gerlingen: Bleicher, 1995.
Niewyk, Donald L. & Francis Nicosia. *The Columbia Guide to the Holocaust.* New York: Columbia University Press, c. 2000.
Schwartz, Mimi. *Good Neighbors, Bad Times: Echoes of my Father's German Village.* Lincoln: University of Nebraska Press, 2008.
Scrase, David & Wolfgang Mieder (eds.), *The Holocaust. Personal Accounts.* Burlington, Vermont: Center for Holocaust Studies, 2001.

A Jewish Quest for Belonging:
Ruth Beckermann's Film *The Paper Bridge* (1987)

Helga Schreckenberger

Introduction

The twentieth annual Harry H. Kahn Memorial Lecture was presented on April 6, 2009, and we were honored to have our very own colleague Prof. Helga Schreckenberger from the Department of German and Russian at the University of Vermont as our distinguished speaker. For over twenty years she has been a major voice for various social issues on our campus, distinguishing herself in a number of administrative positions, including her directorship of Women's Studies and her chairpersonship of her home department.

It is indeed with much pleasure and excitement that I would like to introduce this afternoon's speaker to you who is well known to all of us here on the campus of the University of Vermont. Prof. Helga Schreckenberger stems from Vienna, Austria, but she came to the United States in order to pursue graduate studies, earning two M.A. degrees in German and French in 1980 and 1984 respectively and the Ph.D. degree in 1985 from the University of Kansas in Lawrence, Kansas. After having taught for one year at Bryn Mawr College, it was our good fortune to attract her to the University of Vermont, where she was promoted to Associate Professor with tenure in 1992 and subsequently to Full Professor of German in 2000. Ever since her arrival on our campus she has been a treasured colleague and professor, and all members of the Department of German and Russian are extremely pleased to have her as the chairperson of our vibrant and valuable Department of German and Russian.

Even just a cursory glance at Prof. Schreckenberger's *curriculum vitae* reveals that she is a very engaged and committed scholar, teacher, and administrator. Regarding her impeccable scholarship, it should be noted that she is the co-author (with Peter Ensberg) of a book on *Gerhard Roth: Kunst als Auflehnung gegen das Sein* (1994) and the editor of two valuable essay volumes entitled *Die Ästhetiken des Exils* (2003) and *Die Alchemie des Exils. Exil als schöpferischer Impuls* (2005). Together with her colleague and friend Jacqueline Vansant she has undertaken the difficult task of translating two of Gerhard Roth's novels, thereby making *The Calm Ocean* (1993) and *The Story of Darkness* (1999) by this modern Austrian author accessible to English readers. While Prof. Schreckenberger is clearly one of the experts on Gerhard Roth, having also published numerous articles on him, her expertise in Austrian literature is, of course, much broader than that. There are many articles on major Austrian writers, among them Lilian Faschinger, Otto Grünmandl, Wolf Haas, Peter Handke, Marie Thérèse Kerschbaumer, Joseph Roth, Marlene Streeruwitz, Heinz R. Unger, and Vladimir Vertlib. In addition to her published work on fellow Austrians, Prof. Schreckenberger is one of the key-players in representing Austrian culture, language, and literature here in the United States, to wit her leadership role as the Vice President (2004-2006) and then President (2006-2008) of the Modern Austrian Literature and Culture Association and her long-time service as book review editor (1999-2006) for the journal *Modern Austrian Literature*. In addition, she has organized one of the annual meetings of the Modern Austrian Literature and Culture Association, and as one would expect, she is a speaker on cultural, literary, and sociopolitical matters related to Austria at several conferences a year both here and in Europe.

Another area in which Prof. Schreckenberger is internationally known is the study of exile literature, and it is here where her work also deals with the Holocaust as reflected in modern literary works. Some of her remarkable articles include "Erich Maria Remarque im amerikanischen Exil" (1998). "Die politische Rednerin: Erika Mann im amerikanischen Exil" (2001) "Vortragstätigkeit der Exilschriftsteller in den USA" (2002), "'Heimat,' Exile, and Modernity in Carl Zuckmayer's *Vermonter Roman*" (2008), and "Aimless Travels: Deromanticizing Exile in Irmgard Keun's *Kind aller Länder*" (2009). Additional articles deal with such exiled writers as Franziska Ascher-Nash, Joseph Hahn, Arnold Zweig, and many others. As expected, Prof. Schrecken-berger has served as the president of the Exile Literature Society since 2000, and she has presented innumerable lectures in various countries.

Since all good things come in threes, it should not be surprising that there is at least one more major field of inquiry in which Prof. Schreckenberger continues to excel on the national and international level. From 2000 until 2007 she was the director of Women's Studies at the University of Vermont, and this commitment to the study of women has informed both her teaching and scholarship. There are two fascinating articles on how women experienced World War I, while others deal with alienation, sexual politics, and other gender specific issues. Again she has lectured in Austria, Canada, Germany, and the United States on these topics, and in 2003 she had the exciting opportunity to travel to Havana, Cuba, to give a lecture on "Integrating a Global Perspective into Women's Studies Curriculum" that grew directly out of her teaching and administrative work at the University of Vermont. Another memorable trip in 2005 was to the University of Lodz in Poland, where Prof. Schreckenberger talked about "Frauen an der Front: Der Erste Weltkrieg und seine Konsequenzen für weibliches Selbstverständis."

It should also be mentioned that Prof. Schreckenberger has a keen interest in how ethnocentricity could give way to multiculturalism. Again she has published on this topic, and her work was honored by a large award by the National Endowment for the Humanities, giving Prof. Schreckenberger the opportunity to hold a seminar during the summer of 2006 on "Melting Pot Vienna, Now and Then" in her very own home town. Naturally there are numerous other honors, notably the Outstanding UVM Faculty Woman Award (2007) and various grants to support her research and travels to major conferences, including those held by the Modern Language Association of America, the American Association of Teachers of German, the German Studies Association, the Society for German-American Studies, and the Modern Austrian Literature and Culture Association.

By now it is clear that Prof. Schreckenberger has unlimited energy, enthusiasm, commitment, and intellectual curiosity. In ad-

dition, she is a wonderful mother of two children, with her son
Lukas being a student at the University of Vermont and her
daughter Zoe hopefully coming here as well in a few years. It is
truly amazing to reflect on the accomplishments of this invaluable
colleague, and I have not even mentioned her presidency of the
Northern New England Chapter of the American Association of
Teachers of German (1987-1989, 1995-1996), her organization of
an International Symposium on German Exile Literature at the
University of Vermont (1998), and her many committee assign-
ments over the years, among them the President's Commission for
Lesbian, Gay, Bisexual, and Transgender Equity (2003-2006), the
Faculty Standards Committee (1994-1996, 1999, 2004-2007), the
President's Commission on the Status of Women (1994-1996),
and her service as the Director of the German House (1986-1992).
But let me stop here, hoping that I have been able to do justice to
Prof. Schreckenberger's accomplishments in this short review of
her scholarship. teaching, and service to the profession. Suffice it
to say finally that she is a truly remarkable colleague, instructor,
and friend, recognized nationally and internationally by her peers,
but valued and admired at the University of Vermont by all of us
and especially also by her eager students for whom Prof. Schreckenberger is a living and engaging role model.

Prof. Helga Schreckenberger has made a giant difference on
our campus and elsewhere for many years, and she will most certainly also intrigue and enrich us with her lecture.

Lecture[1]
"Who are we, the Jews of the Second Generation? What dis-
tinguishes us?"[2]   These are questions central to Ruth Beckermann's autobiographical documentary *Die papierene Brücke*
(The Paper Bridge), a film that takes us to the region of former
Bukovina in Eastern Europe, to Israel, and returns to Vienna with
an exploration of Jewish life there.[3] Implicit in this inquiry about
the Second Generation is the question of their belonging. Beckermann calls the film not without irony a "Heimatsuche auf
Jüdisch"—"Jewish Quest for Belonging/Home."[4]   Her explicit
presence in the film, both as narrator and interviewer underscore
the personal nature of this quest. *The Paper Bridge* thus represents

the Austrian filmmaker's struggle to define and understand her particular identity as a Viennese Jew and as a member of her generation, the children of Holocaust Survivors. I would like to preface my analysis of Beckermann's film by situating it within the post-World War II Austrian socio-political and cultural landscape, specifically paying attention to what it meant to be Jewish in postwar Austria.

I. Beckermann's film in the context of post World War II Austria

In the period following World War II, Germany and Austria underwent distinctly different socio-historical developments which in turn shaped the cultural production of the two countries. The National Socialist past influenced both the constitution and politics of the post-war German Republic. Germany officially accepted its role in the mass murder of European Jewry and the government consciously sought a break with the past. Austria, however, with the aid of the Moscow declaration of 1943 presented itself convincingly as Hitler's first victim. Thus, it abdicated any complicity in the holocaust as well as any responsibility for its surviving Jewish citizens. One example is the government's unwillingness to provide restitution or to return "Aryanized" property to its rightful owners.

This different social reality is reflected in the literature of both countries. While the fascist past and its lingering influence on persisting authoritarian structures emerged as a dominant topic in German literature in the sixties, attention to this past occurred in Austrian literature first in the eighties. The catalyzing event was undoubtedly the presidential nomination and subsequent election of the former UN-Secretary General Kurt Waldheim in 1986. Accusations concerning Waldheim's military service in the Balkans and Greece, especially his knowledge of the murder of thousands of Yugoslav Partisans and the deportation of Greek Jews to concentration camps in the East surfaced during the presidential campaign.[5] These revelations divided the country and initiated a new wave of anti-Semitism that proved beyond a doubt how ill prepared the Austrian public was for an honest look at their past personal and collective guilt. These events surrounding Waldheim's candidacy moved many Austrians, including elected officials like Chancellor Vranitzky, to reflect upon the official historical ac-

count of the past and the embarrassing consequences of denial
and amnesia. Austria's National Socialist past, and its way of
dealing with its legacy increasingly became a topic for both Jewish and Non-Jewish Austrian writers and artists.

For Jewish Austrians, the Waldheim affair and the ensuing
resurgence of a public anti-Semitic discourse signaled their renewed displacement from the ranks of "real" Austrians. This presented a reason to examine their identity as Jews and Austrians
and reflect upon their situation in a country that for a long time
had ignored or at least marginalized the experiences of its Jewish
citizens.

II. Being Jewish in post World War II Austria

Before the Anschluss (Austria's so-called annexation by Nazi
Germany), about 200,000 Jews lived in Austria, almost 90% of
them lived in Vienna. Anti-Semitism in Vienna was both racially
and religiously motivated and politically instrumentalized by the
right-wing parties including the German Nationals and the Christian Socialists. In contrast to National Socialism, the pre-war anti-
Semitic politicians did not aim to hurt the Jews but to blame them
for economical crisis.[6] With the rise of Hitler and the National
Socialists, anti-Semitism also turned more aggressive in Austria.
Active persecution of started in March 1938 with the Anschluss.
The historian John Bunzl speaks of an "anti-Semitic need to catch
up" ("antisemitischer Nachholbedarf") on the part of the Viennese
population whose hatred against the Jews had been promoted by
the political right for decades.[7] They not only participated whole-
heartedly in the physical abuse and degradation of Jews but also
in their dispossession. In a short period of time, 70,000 apart-
ments and 25% of all businesses were repossessed by "Aryans."[8]

A third of the Jewish Austrians were murdered or perished in
concentration camps, 126,500 were forced to immigrate; a few
were able to survive in hiding. Today, about 10,000 Jews live in
Austria forming a demographically very diverse community.
They are made up of survivors of concentration camps, their children, displaced persons or refugees from Poland, Hungary, Rumania and the former Soviet Union. It is estimated that only between
3,500 to 4,500 of the émigrés returned to Vienna.[9] In 1945 both
holocaust survivors and rémigrés were regarded as undesirable by

the Austrian population and the government. They had to overcome the obstacles of an unhelpful, unbending bureaucracy to gain legal status, and were repeatedly confronted with the undiminished anti-Semitism of the population. Moreover, the efforts of the government to establish a positive Austrian national identity based on the victim-myth mandated that the Jewish existence and Jewish experience be rendered invisible. The presence of the Jews was an unwelcome reminder of a past that the dominant culture was eager of forgets. Those who wanted to remain or return had to do so as Austrians, and not as Jews. A prominent example is the extremely popular Austrian Chancellor Bruno Kreisky who always defined himself as a Social Democrat and an Austrian first and had the "delicacy" never to remind his countrymen of the losses he and his family sustained during the Holocaust.

As the sociologist Christoph Reinprecht points out in his study *Returned. Identity and Rupture in the Biography of Austrian Jews (Zurückgekehrt. Identität und Bruch in der Biographie österreichischer Juden)*, under such circumstances, it was shear impossible for Jewish reemigres to Austria to establish a positive Jewish identity:

> *They returned as isolated individuals but were perceived by the others as scattered parts of an imagined collective. At this level, their Jewishness, their Jewish identity was not self-determined but projected upon them. It was fixed for those affected-in form of the historical fact of persecution and destruction that was part of their experience and it was fixed in the narrow framework of the social conditions of postwar Austria. At the same time, it was not possible to revert to traditional patterns of identification [...] because in Austria, a self-confident and as such "normal" Jewish identity was not possible anymore.[10]*

The forced identification with an imagined collective on one hand and the impossibility to enact traditional roles associated with that collective on the other hand led many remigres to withdraw from public life, to become invisible. In her collection of essays *Excluded: Austrians and Jews after 1945 (Unzugehörig: Österreicher und Juden nach 1945)*, Ruth Beckerman states: "In order to

live in Vienna, Jews had to follow certain stipulations which were·
repress your own history; consider the case closed. Begin at
ground zero. Pretend as if all that were possible."[11] Beckermann
aims her criticism not only at the dominant culture that imposes
such stipulations but also at the parent generation who accepted
such limitations and complied tacitly with the official version of
Austrian history promoted by the post-war government.

This silence, repression and exclusion of the parent generation were not lost on the next generation. Beckermann relates how
for her and other Jewish Austrians of her generation, growing up
Jewish in Vienna was an ambivalent experience. Statements like:
"My childhood is located in a no-man's land," "We lived here, yet
not here" or "Home was an extraterritorial zone"[12] communicate
their sense of dislocation.

Beckermann and many of her generation attempted to overcome their isolation by rejecting their parents and their expectations for them. They became deeply involved with first Zionism
then the political left with whom they believed to share strong an-
tifascist convictions. However, their political activism still meant
the suppression of their Jewish identity. In addition, it became
complicated by the anti-Semitic undertones of the anti-Zionism of
the left. In the eighties, coinciding with the Waldheim-affair,
Beckermann and other Jewish Austrians broke with the left and
turned their attention to their Jewish identity:

> *"For the first time we began to make a connection be-
> tween our relationship to our parents and the Jewish fate
> and to examine it. This was not to be understood as a re-
> bellion but as an attempt to comprehend the dimension of
> the rupture which had occurred before our birth and
> which determined our life. The political disappointment
> was only one trigger. As important was our own age and
> that of the generation of the survivors. And the distance
> to the events themselves which after forty years surfaced
> as memories."[13]*

In my discussion of Beckermann's film *The Paper Bridge* I will
demonstrate that it grew out of her examination of the Second
generations' place within Jewish history and their role in carrying

on the memory work of the Holocaust survivor generation.

III. *The Paper Bridge*

Like most of her other films, *The Paper Bridge* is an example of Ruth Beckermann's very personal approach to documentary film making. In the production notes to the film, Beckermann explains that she was attempting to transgress the narrow confines of the documentary film: Since the completion of [the film] *Return to Vienna* I am contemplating the possibility to find forms on the margins of the documentary film that allow to use language not simply as commentary and images not alone as evidence. The connection between image and language should be made on a different, deeper, more complex level."[14] She chose the less restrictive form of the film essay, a genre which according to Philip Lopate allows the filmmaker to ask questions without necessary finding solutions but "enacting the struggle for truth in full view."[15] All of the characteristics Lopate ascribes to the film essay apply to *The Paper Bridge*: In the film we find a connection between words and images, a unified voice, eloquence, a central tension or argument, and a personal point of view.[16]

This more subjective stance of the film essay allows Beckermann to blur the boundaries between history and memory, between the personal and the collective.[17] This becomes clear when we consider Beckermann's exploration of the elements which she sees as defining for her and her generation. They include the specific situation of the Jews in Austria, the eradication of an Eastern European Jewish tradition, the holocaust, and finally, Zionism.[18] Beckermann reflects on these disparate elements of Jewish experiences by connecting them to her personal history. She does this visually through the shot of her reflection in a shop window. The multiplied, fragmented mirror image of the filmmaker suggests the incompatibility of these elements. Since the image is a reflection of herself, Beckermann reveals her own identity as problematic and fragmented.

The film develops into a journey to reconcile the different fragments of her identity, a quest that takes her from Vienna to Bukowina and back. The film starts out in Vienna in a setting that emphasizes Beckermann's feeling of not-belonging. The very first images set in Beckermann's attic apartment in a former Jewish section of the inner city capture a feeling of isolation, of disconcerting limbo that she describes in her essay about her childhood in Vienna. We see an empty apartment whose windows are covered with netting because of an ongoing renovation. The noise from the streets is muffled because of the protective hangings that at the same time isolate the narrator—Beckermann from the outside world. The images as well as the accompanying narrative recreate the feeling of extraterritoriality that Beckermann associates with her childhood.

Following the scenes of the apartment, Beckermann explains in a voice-over what motivated her to undertake the film project: She spent the entire summer reflecting on her family history, looking at old photographs, and asking her relatives questions, yet, as she states: "I gained no further understanding this summer."[19] Both, the spoken and the visual narratives of the film suggest that it is impossible for Beckermann to find answers to her questions in Vienna. Her situation is visualized in a sequence taken from the inside of a streetcar that circles the inner city of Vienna. Just like the streetcar circling a center, but never arriving, Beckermann too is literally going in circles.[20]

Since the city does not answer her questions concerning the past or the present, Beckermann leaves Vienna for the Bukovina, the area of the one-time Austro-Hungarian Monarchy from where her father immigrated to Vienna after the war.[21] As Christina Guenther points out, Beckermann "reverses the trajectory of her forebears who, traveling westward arrived as hopeful immigrants in Vienna from the eastern margins of the Habsburg Empire."[22] This reversal suggests a return to the roots of Jewish existence, an existence that is not distorted by assimilation and silence but rather, a self-evident, un-questioning Jewish identity. Moreover, the places and people Beckermann encounters in the cities of Sereth, Radautz and Sutschara recall stories she's heard from her childhood.

Beckermann's desire to integrate the scenes and images she encounters with her memories and imagination dominate her exploration of the landscape. She visits the Yiddish-speaking local rabbi, the only kosher butcher left in the region who recalls for her the stories about the "Wunderrabbi of Sadagura" related to her by her father. The memories and stories of her childhood come alive even as Beckermann only finds traces of a formerly active Jewish community in the cities of Sereth, Radautz, and Sutschara, communities now threatened with extinction as its older members die and its young members emigrate. The signs are unmistakable. The Jewish community of Radautz consists of only ten men, all advanced in years, the traditional bathhouse is not used by the Jewish community any longer but by peasant women from the area. The Hanukkah celebration at the synagogue of another village has drawn a large and lively audience that is welcoming to the visitors "who just want to take a quick look at where they come from, where their parents and grandparents and all of their stories came from"[23] but here too all talks turn to emigration to Israel and the Hebrew teacher has only two students. Only the giant Jewish cemeteries of the region are left to testify to the former size of the Jewish community. The many tombstones are both evidence of Jewish community life and of its extinction. Moreover, they also remind us of the millions of Jews murdered in the concentration camps that were not granted a grave but died in anonymity.

The loss of community is also reflected by the camera's long focus on an empty landscape that concludes the journey to the Bukovina. In retrospect, the cutting down of a huge old tree which Beckermann films at her arrival in the Bukovina can be interpreted as a metaphor for the fate of the Jewish people. The violent severing of the tree from its roots symbolically represents the consequences of the Holocaust while the images of tree trunks being dispersed either by boat or by cart that reappear several times in the film, indicate the continuing uprooting and fragmentation of the Jewish people.

As the film suggests, Beckermann cannot repossess her heritage by returning to its geographical location. But she can preserve and recuperate the forgotten stories and histories of these vanishing communities.

Beckermann then turns her attention to another possibility of Jewish identity—Zionism. The following scenes of the film are shot in Israel, which has remained a country of identification as well as destination of emigration for many members of the postwar generation. The images of the modern, urban Israel present a stark contrast to the seemingly archaic Eastern European Jewish communities. In Israel too, childhood memories intrude into the

present. Beckermann's mother came to Israel after she was forced
to leave Vienna at age fourteen. Similar to the father's idealized
memories of the Bukovina, Beckermann's mother's recollections
of Israel are only positive. Israel represents to her "the country
that saved her," the "land of liberation."[24] Beckermann does not
share her mother's uncritical view of Israel. Like the Orthodox Judaism of the Eastern European communities with its gendered
spaces, Israel's militaristic Zionism does not offer her the spiritual home she is looking for. In Israel she sees herself put to the
choice: "Assimilation or Aliyah: Ascent into the land of single opportunity."[25] For Beckermann that would mean to give up Jewry
to become an Israeli.

The journey to both the Bukovina and Israel suggests that for
Beckermann, overcoming her feeling of not-belonging involves
returning to her parent's roots, understanding their history and applying her new-found knowledge to her own situation. In her production notes to *The Paper Bridge*, she writes: "I not only wanted to follow the few traces of my family's history but also wanted to find out how these often told stories blend with my experiences and feelings."[26] Beckermann not only wants to document
history or only her parent's history, but she also seeks to locate her
own place in this story. The Bukovina and Israel are places of be-
longings for her parents, but as she discovers not for her.

Constructing her identity through her parents' biography, she
can only use these memories to negotiate an identity for herself in
her own space of belonging. Thus after exploring the geographical and spiritual places of her Jewish heritage, Beckermann returns to Vienna, examining it as the place where her parents chose
to settle. The sociologist Christoph Reinprecht emphasizes in his
study the importance of the Second Generation's understanding
of the motives that caused their parents to return to a country that
participated in their persecution: "This inability to understand the
"existential decision" of the parents plays an important role in the
formation of their own identity and their own Jewish self-image
and self-consciousness."[27] In *The Paper Bridge*, this topic occu-
pies a prominent space. Beckermann inserts extended conversations with her parents into the film where they discuss the reasons
for their return to Vienna or, in the case of the father, reasons for
his decision to settle there.

For Beckermann's mother, Vienna remains the city from which she was forced to escape as a child under the threat of death and Austria remains the country where a majority of her family was murdered. She continues to identify with Israel where she spent an important part of her youth. Out of her love for her husband, who could not imagine life in Israel, she consented to return to Vienna. While she calls her life in Vienna "pleasant" and praises its rich cultural offerings, returning to this city remains a source of emotional conflict for Beckermann's mother. She feels a great deal of guilt towards her children because she considers Austria unsafe for them.

In contrast to the pessimistic view of his wife, Beckermann's father has developed a positive relationship to Austria. He only came to the country after the war in order to escape life under the Soviet rule. Beckermann's father still maintains idealizing memories of his place of birth in the Bukovina and its cultural center Chernowitz which at that time was part of the Habsburg Empire. He tells stories of the respectful and harmonic co-existence of all members of the different ethnic and religious groups and of the lack of any anti-Semitic sentiments. These memories are at the bottom of his unwavering faith in the civilized Habsburg Reich and its center, Vienna. This faith led him to come to Vienna and it continues to define his love for the city. Even now he keeps a picture of the Emperor Franz Josef hanging in his office, pointing to his lingering positive associations with the Habsburg monarchy.

In her essay collection, *Excluded*, Beckermann describes this idealizing attitude towards Vienna with analytic distance:

The Eastern European Jews who after 1945 constituted the majority of the Viennese Jewish community do not associate their traumatic experiences with Vienna but with Ukrainian and Romanian fascists, Hungarian Arrow crosses and German-speaking Nazis. They didn't experience prewar Austrian Anti-Semitism and the behavior of the population after the Anschluß. To the contrary, they brought their romantically idealized image of the Empire's capital with them despite the collapse of the monarchy (101).[28]

Beckermann sees the positive identification of the Eastern European Jews with the Habsburg monarchy continue in the post-war period:

It also seems to be no coincidence that the Jews who remained in Vienna after the liberation, chose for their favorite meeting places exactly those places that corresponded to their image of the former monarchy such as: the Meierei in the Stadtpark, the Cobenzl and the Semmering. The Habsburg architecture became the backdrop for the meetings of a patchwork group of people with a similar prewar experience and a similar fate during the Nazi-regime.[29]

Beckermann understands the reasons for her father's love of Vienna but also recognizes that it is built on its specious premise. It leads to a similar nostalgic and uncritical relationship to the past that she observes in other Viennese Holocaust survivors in postwar Austria:

They mythologize their own history, clinging to the great musicians and poets that Jewish Vienna produced, while forgetting the dark side of emancipation and assimilation. They fantasize that they are back in the idealized past, without admitting to themselves that it was this past that led to the era of National Socialist persecution.[30]

This idealization of the past, in particular the fin-de-siècle, the continued identification with the Habsburg monarchy seems to offer the parent generation the psychological means to cope with the present. However, they are recreating a past that is rooted in transfigured nostalgia and as such obscures the reality of the war and the Holocaust.[31]

In contrast to her father and others of his generation, Beckermann's view of the turn of the century is understandably more critical. Her camera captures the monument of Karl Lueger in front of Café Pruckl, a coffee house reminiscent of the famous Jewish coffee house culture of the fin-de-siècle. Lueger, the turn of the century Viennese mayor famous for his anti-Semitism

which he deftly instrumentalized for political gain serves as a reminder of the precarious situation of the Jews in this city past and
present. These images not only reflect Beckermann's ambivalent
feelings towards Vienna but also question the romantic and idealized image of Vienna held by the East European Jews and her father.

When she interviews her father in the film, he dismisses the
recurrent anti-Semitism of the Viennese as limited to a certain
kind of people and he asserts his ability to deal with such occur-
rences if necessary even with force. The film offers a more pessimistic view of the state of Viennese anti-Semitism. Beckermann's interview with her father is intercut with contemporary
footage of an anti-Waldheim demonstration in the inner city of Vienna where supporters and opponents of the candidate come to
blows. We see the police breaking up the demonstration and ar-
resting one of the demonstrators who insists on his right to protest
against Waldheim. Beckermann's father appears in the segment
confronting Waldheim supporters, which unleashes a belligerent
stream of anti-Semitic vulgarities. Ironically, Beckermann asks in
a voice-over "Who says that the Viennese don't recognize Jews
anymore? They unmasked my father as a Jew instantly"[32]

The five-minute long scene, filmed with a handheld video
camera, makes it shockingly clear how easily old prejudices were
resurrected and that it was permissible again in the eighties to
openly and freely express anti-Semitic feelings and convictions.
The possibility to develop a positive and confident Jewish-Austrian identity in such a charged atmosphere seems questionable.
Rather it suggests the renewed displacement of Viennese Jews
from the rank of "real" Austrians.

Beckermann does not limit her probe to the experiences of her
family but includes those of other Viennese Jews. The two seg-
ments of the film, the trip to the Bukovina and the scenes in Vienna are separated by Beckermann's side-journey to Osijek, in the
former Yugoslavia. It is the location of the Hollywood production
of Hermann Wouk's novel *War and Remembrance*. The production crew had erected a model of Theresienstadt and had engaged
"authentic Jews" from Vienna as extras for the film. Ruth Beckermann focuses on the motives that caused these men and women
of both the survivor and second generation to make themselves

available as so-called "extras of the Jewish fate."[33] While for the older generation, the participation in the film leads to a confrontation of their own memories and trauma, for the younger generation it is an attempt to reenact and thus understand the experiences of their parents. The camera captures discussions among the participants as well as those moments when long suppressed memories surface irrevocably in face of the mountains of corpses made of cardboard. Both generations are still defined by the past; their vulnerability is made tangible by the film. As Hillary Herzog points out, "Unable to tell their own stories in a city that long made these stories taboo, they end up as extras in a American version of their story-a narrative only possible because of the spatial and temporal distance that Americans have to the Holocaust, a distance that is impossible for Austrian Jews.[34] Ironically, it is the unreal space of the film set that makes memories possible. For the survivors, the repressed past surfaces in the present, surprisingly and unexpectedly. Thus, the film set turns into a site of memory and exchange of stories.[35] However, the past also intrudes in shape of old clichés and prejudices. The make-up artist makes sure that the Jews are looking Jewish enough and a Jewish woman who recently immigrated to Vienna from the former Soviet Union tells about the prejudices she encounters from the Viennese Jews.

The film ends in Vienna, back in Beckermann's apartment in the first district indicating that she is ready to re-appropriate her place as an Austrian Jew within this city. Her ambivalence towards Vienna remains unresolved creating a tension that will remain a driving force for Beckermann's continued critical engagement with her heritage and her position in the present. Again, the camera captures images of the Ringstrasse from inside the streetcar. While the narrator describes Vienna as a city to which she reacts with joy, she juxtaposes images to this narrative, suggesting a tension between the narrator and the city. As the narrator expresses the joy the city brings her, we see the Hofburg and the Heldenplatz where Hitler was received by an enthusiastic Viennese population. Vienna remains the ambivalent space where familiarity and comfort co-exist in tension with the sense of not-belonging. This tension however is the prerequisite for continuous intellectual engagement with the city, its history, and it's present.

The very last images of the film show a series of photographs of Beckermann's family, her parents, grandparents, siblings, and herself as a small girl. Forming a bridge, these photographs remind us of the title of the film the meaning of which is explained by the tale of mythic storyteller Hagazussa. She tells of two bridges in a village on the river Pruth, one made of iron and one made of cigarette paper. The townspeople choosing the iron bridge fall into the river and perish while those who trust in the paper bridge reach safety on the other shore. Hagazussa's story can be understood as follow: the paper bridge symbolizes that paper that captures stories and images, brings them back to life, records them and keeps them from being forgotten. The paper bridge also connects the past with the present and thus, the different generations. However, like the paper bridge, the connection is fragile and needs to be treated with care. Beckermann's film is such a paper bridge that commemorates and preserves her Jewish heritage by recuperation forgotten stories, images and photographs thus forging the connection between past and the present.

Beckermann's film is above all a critical examination of the heritage conveyed to her by her parents and their memories. She attempts to blend this legacy with her own experience in the present. The journey into the past provides her with answers about the past and allows her to accept her ambivalence towards her Jewish-Austrian identity. *The Paper Bridge* thus convincingly conveys the necessity for the Second Generation to look to past of the survivor generation as they contemplate their identity/place in Austria society. However, the film also rejects the notion of a fixed Jewish identity rooted within a specific geographical location. Constructing identity entails, so the film suggests, an ongoing critical engagement with the present and a continuous building of bridges to the past.

Notes:

[1] I would like to express my gratitude to Jacqueline Vansant for her excellent editorial suggestions.

[2] Ruth Beckermann, *Die papierene Brücke*. The quotations from the film correspond to the English subtitles.

[3] The film was shown with great success at numerous European film festivals. It received "Das goldene Einhorn," an award

for best documentary film at the Alpinade in Bludenz, Vorarlberg (Austria).

4 Ruth Beckermann, *Die papierene Brücke.*

5 An investigation by an international commission of historians, appointed by the Austrian government, found that there was no proof of Waldheim's direct involvement in these atrocities However, the commission raised sincere doubts that Wald could have been ignorant of these events as he continued to claim. (See Simon Wiesenthal, "The Waldheim Case," in *Contemporary Jewish Writing in Austria* ed. by Dagmar Lorenz. Lincoln: Universityof Nebraska Press, 1999, 81-95.

6 See Christoph Reinprecht, *Zurückgekehrt. Identität und Bruch in der Biographie österreichischer Juden.* Wien: Braumüller, 1992, 28.

7 John Bunzl, "Zur Geschichte des Antisemitismus in Österreich" in: *Antisemitismus in Österreich*, ed. John Bunzl and Bernd Marin. Innsbruck: Inn-Verlag, 1983, 9-88, here 60.

8 See Reinprecht, 28.

9 See Reinprecht, 29.

10 Christoph Reinprecht, *Zurückgekehrt. Identität und Bruch in der Biographie österreichischer Juden.* Wien: Braumüller, 1992, 110: "Sie kamen als isolierte Individuen zurück, wurden aber von den anderen als verspringte Teile eines imaginären Kollektivs wahrgenommen, ihr Jude-Sein, ihre jüdische Identität war auf dieser Ebene somit nicht mehr frei bestimmbar, sondern festgelegt. Und zwar sowohl in den Betroffenen selbst-als die in den Erfahrungshorizont eingekerbte historische Objektivität von Verfolgung und Vernichtung—als auch im engen Rahmen der gesellschaftlichen Verhältnisse im Nachkriegsösterreich. Zugleich aber war die bei Verlust sozialer Rollen naheliegende Fixierung auf tradierte Identifikationsmuster und—angebote verwehrt, eben weil [...] in Österreich ein selbstbewusstes und in diesem Sinne 'normales' jüdisches Selbstverständnis nicht mehr möglich war." All translations are mine if not otherwise indicated.)

11 Ruth Beckermann, "Ausgerechnet Wien?" in: *Unzugehörig. Juden und Österreicher nach 1945.* Wien: Loecker, 1989, 111: "Um in Wien zu leben, mußten sich die Juden auf Bedingungen einlassen, die heißen: Verdrängen der eigenen Geschichte. Die Rechnung als abgeschlossen betrachten. Bei Null anfangen.

So tun, als wäre das möglich."
[12] Beckermann, "Jugend in Wien" in: Unzugehörig, 117:
"'Meine Kindheit liegt in einem Niemandsland.? 'Wir lebten hier
und doch nicht hier.' 'Zu Hause, das war exterritoriales Gebiet.?"
[13] Ibid., 126: "Zum ersten Mal begannen wir, die Verstrickung
unserer Beziehung zu den Eltern mit dem judischen Schicksal zu
erforschen. Nicht als Rebellion, sondern als Versuch das Ausmaß
des Bruches zu begreifen, der vor unserer Geburt entstanden war
und unser Leben prägte. Dabei war die poliltische Enttäuschung
nur ein auslösendes Moment. Eine mindestens so wichtige Rolle
spielte das eigene Lebensalter und das der Generation der Über-
lebenden. Und der zeitliche Abstand zu den Ereignissen selbst,
die nach vierzig Jahren als Erinnerung wieder auftauchten."
[14] Ruth Beckerman, "Zur Produktion." (Unpublished, part of
the press kit entitled "Die papierene Brücke. Ein Film von Ruth
Beckermann"): "Seit der Fertigstellung von WIEN RETOUR
beschäftige ich mich mit der Möglichkeit, Formen im Grenzbe-
reich des Dokumentarfilms zu finden, die es erlauben, die
Sprache nicht als Kommentar und die Bilder nicht allein als Be-
weisstücke einzusetzen. Der Zusammenhang von Bild und
Sprache soll auf einer anderen, tiefer gelegenen und vielschichti-
gen Ebene hergestellt werden."
[15] Philip Lopate, "In Search of the Centaur: The Essay-Film"
in: *Beyond Document: Essays on Nonfiction Film*, ed. by Charles
Warren. Hanover, New Hampshire: Wesleyan University Press,
1996, 243-270, here 245.
[16] See Lopate, 246-247.
[17] Hillary Herzog ("The Global and the Local in Ruth Beckermann's Films and Writings" in: *Rebirth of a Culture. Jewish
Identity and Jewish Writing in Germany and Austria Today*, ed. by
Hillary Hope Herzog, Todd Herzog and Benjamin Lapp. New
York: Berghahn, 2008, 100-109) remarks also: "The boundaries
between history and memory, between the personal and the collective are fluid in this film." (104).
[18] See "Zur Produktion."
[19] Beckermann, *The Paper Bridge*.
[20] See also Herzog, 103.
[21] The Bukovina was the crown land farthest to the East of the
Habsburg Empire. Its multi-ethnic population consisting of Ro-

manians, Poles, Ruthenians, Germans, Jews, Hungarians and Armenians co-existed relatively peacefully. The Bukovina is known for its rich cultural heritage which grew out of this incredible diversity. Joseph Roth, Paul Celan or Rosa Ausländer are the best known examples of Jewish authors from this area who enriched German literature. Today, the region straddles the boundary between Rumania and the Ukraine.
[22] Christa Guenther, "The Politics of Location in Ruth Beckermann's 'Vienna Films.'" *Modern Austrian Literature* 37, 3/4 (2004) 33-46, here 37
[23] Beckermann, *Die papierene Brücke.*
[24] Beckermann, *Die papierene Brücke.*
[25] Ibid.
[26] Beckermann, "Zur Produktion": "Ich wollte nicht nur die wenigen Spuren meiner Familiengeschichte nachgehen, sondern herausfinden, wie sich die erwiesenen und erzählten Geschichten mit meinen eigenen Erlebnissen und Gefühlen vermischen."
[27] Reinprecht, 78.
[28] Beckermann, "Ausgerechnet Wien?", 101: "Die osteuropäischen Juden, die nach 1945 die Mehrheit der Wiener Gemeinde bildeten, hatten ihre traumatischen Erfahrungen nicht hier vor Ort gemacht, sondern mit urkainischen und rumänischen Faschisten, ungarischen Pfeilkreuzlern und deutsch-sprechenden Nazis. Sie hatten keine Vorkriegserfahrungen mit dem österreichischen Antisemitismus und dem Verhalten der Bevölkerung nach dem Anschluß. Sie brachten im Gegenteil ein romantisch verklärtes Bild von der Kaiserstadt mit, die für sie auch nach dem Zerfall der Monarchie Anziehungspunkt geblieben war."
[29] Ibid., 102: "Es scheint auch kein Zufall zu sein, daß für die Juden, die nach der Befreiung in Wien blieben, gerade Orte zu beliebten Treffpunkten wurden, die ihrem Bild der ehemaligen Monarchie entsprachen, wie die Meierei im Stadtpark, der Cobenzl und der Semmering. Schönbrunnergelbe Architektur bildete die Kulisse, vor der man sich mit einer zusammengeflickten Verwandtschaftsgruppe von Menschen mit ähnlicher Vorkriegserfahrung und ähnlichem Schicksal während der Nazi-Herrschaft traf."
[30] Beckermann, "Illusionen und Kompromisse," in *Unzugehörig*, 109: Sie mythisieren ihre eigene Geschichte, klammern

sich an die großen Musiker und Dichter, die das jüdische Wien hervorgebracht hat, und vergessen die Schattenseiten von Emanzipation und Assimilation. Sie phantasieren sich zurück in das geschönte Vorgestern, ohne sich klarzumachen, daß es das Vorgesten war, das zum Gestern der nationalsozialistischen Verfolgung führte."

[31] See also Hillary Herzog , 102.

[32] Beckermann, *Die papierene Brücke.*

[33] Beckermann, *Die papierene Brücke.*

[34] Herzog, 106.

[35] See Ibid.